Multinationals, the State, and the Management of Economic Nationalism

MULTINATIONALS, THE STATE, AND THE MANAGEMENT OF ECONOMIC NATIONALISM

_____The Case of Trinidad

CHAITRAM SINGH

PRAEGER

New York
Westport, Connecticut
London

Library of Congress Cataloging-in-Publication Data

Singh, Chaitram.
    Multinationals, the state, and the management of economic
nationalism : the case of Trinidad / Chaitram Singh.
        p.   cm.
    Bibliography: p.
    Includes index.
    ISBN 0-275-93075-0 (alk. paper)
        1. Petroleum industry and trade—Trinidad and Tobago.
2. International business enterprises—Developing countries—Case
studies.   I. Title.
HD9574.T7S56   1989
333.8'87—dc 19   88-28775

Library of Congress Catalog Card Number: 88-28775
ISBN: 0-275-93075-0

First published in 1989

Praeger Publishers, One Madison Avenue, New York, NY 10010
A division of Greenwood Press, Inc.

Printed in the United States of America

∞

The paper used in this book complies with the
Permanent Paper Standard issued by the National
Information Standards Organization (Z39.48-1984).

10 9 8 7 6 5 4 3 2 1

For my mother, Anjanie Singh,
my brother, Anand,
and the memory of my father, Ranjit Singh

CONTENTS

Tables   ix

Abbreviations   xi

Preface   xiii

1. Multinationals in Small Mineral-producing Countries   1

2. An Open Petroleum Economy   17

3. Organization of the Petroleum Industry in Trinidad   31

4. The Ethnic Basis of Politics in Trinidad   47

5. Nationalization as a Mobilization Strategy   61

6. Multinationals, the State, and the Management of Economic
    Nationalism   83

7. Conclusion   111

    Appendix   123

    Bibliography   125

    Index   135

TABLES

1.1 Priorities of Materials   10

2.1 Comparison of Trinidad with Selected Countries on Some Socioeconomic Indicators   18

2.2 Gross Domestic Product at Current Factor Cost, 1960-1985   19

2.3 Gross Domestic Product at Constant Factor Cost, 1960-1985   21

2.4 Contribution of the Petroleum Sector to GDP at Current Factor Cost, 1960-1985   22

2.5 Export of Petroleum and Petroleum Products, 1962-1983   24

2.6 Central Government Revenues, 1972-1985   25

2.7 Government Participation in Commercial Enterprises as a Percentage of Total Government Revenues, 1973-1983   26

2.8 Government Subsidies as a Percentage of Total Revenues, 1973-1983   27

2.9 Expenditure on Foreign Travel by Trinidadian Residents, 1973-1983   28

3.1 Reserves to Production Ratios, 1962-1985   32

3.2 Production of Crude Petroleum by Company, 1967-1983   35

x / Tables

3.3 Percentage Distribution of Crude Petroleum Production by Company, 1973-1983   36

3.4 Petroleum Mining--Method of Production, 1962-1985   38

3.5 Refinery Throughput, 1967-1984   40

3.6 Analysis of Refinery Output, 1967-1984   41

4.1 Ethnic Composition of the Population of Trinidad and Tobago   49

5.1 Industrial Disputes Involving Stoppages of Work, 1950-1964   66

ABBREVIATIONS

ACDC	Action Committee of Dedicated Citizens
API	American Petroleum Institute
ATSEFWTU	All-Trinidad Sugar Estates and Factory Workers' Trade Union
BP	British Petroleum
BWIA	British West Indian Airways
CNLP	Caribbean National Labor Party
CPTU	Conference of Progressive Trade Unions
DAC	Democratic Action Congress
DEWD	Development and Environmental Works Division
DLP	Democratic Labor Party
FWTU	Federated Workers' Trade Union
GDP	Gross Domestic Product
GNP	Gross National Product
ICFTU	Island-wide Cane Farmers' Trade Union
IRA	Industrial Relations Act
ISA	Industrial Stabilization Act
ISCOTT	Iron and Steel Company of Trinidad and Tobago
MNC	Multinational Corporation
NAMOTI	National Movement for the True Independence of Trinidad and Tobago
NAR	National Alliance for Reconstruction
NJAC	National Joint Action Congress
NPMC	National Petroleum Marketing Company
NTUC	National Trade Union Congress
ONR	Organization for National Reconstruction
OPEC	Organization of Petroleum-Exporting Countries
OWTU	Oilfields Workers' Trade Union
PDP	People's Democratic Party

PNM	People's National Movement
POPPG	Party of Political Progress Groups
SPT	Supplemental Petroleum Tax
SWWTU	Seamen and Waterfront Workers' Trade Union
TICFA	Trinidad Island-wide Cane Farmers' Association
TIWU	Transport and Industrial Workers' Union
TLP	Trinidad Labor Party
TNA	Trinidad Northern Areas
TRINTOC	Trinidad and Tobago Oil Company
TTEC	Trinidad and Tobago Electricity Corporation
TTNA	Trinidad and Tobago National Alliance
ULF	United Labor Force
WASA	Water and Sewage Authority
WIIP	West Indian Independence Party
WFP	Workers' and Farmers' Party

PREFACE

This book examines the opportunities and means available to small mineral-producing Third World countries to improve their bargaining positions with the multinational corporations involved in the extraction of their minerals. Trinidad and Tobago, which is a small producer of petroleum, is used as an illustrative case study.

The field research for this book was conducted in 1982 and 1987. Funding for the 1982 field trip was provided by the Department of Political Science and by the Center for Latin American Studies at the University of Florida. The Institute for Social and Economic Research of the University of the West Indies, St. Augustine, served as the local sponsor for the research. Funding for the 1987 field trip was provided by Berry College. I would like to thank these institutions for their support.

The Appendix lists the names of those individuals in Trinidad who consented to be interviewed. I would like to thank each of them for taking the time from his busy schedule to see me and to respond to my questions. I would also like to thank Pamela Benson, senior librarian at the Ministry of Energy, for providing me with copies of public documents relating to the oil industry.

Many people contributed to making my trips to Trinidad comfortable and productive, and I would like to thank them all, especially Seunarine and Drupatee Persad, Lalchan Singh, Clement and Celina Sankat, Lugard Layne, and Fred and Pauline Hall.

I owe a special debt of gratitude to Eugene R. Wittkopf, Alfred B. Clubok, Terry L. McCoy, Andres Suarez, Alfonso J. Damico, Robert Lawless, and Parsram Singh, all of whom read the manuscript and commented extensively on it.

I reserve special thanks to my wife, Kathy, who accompanied me to Trinidad on the first field trip and proved to be an invaluable asset. Her patience, understanding, encouragement, and support at every step of the way has always been deeply appreciated.

Finally, I wish to thank Kathy Cromer in the Research Department at Berry College for her patience and care in typing several drafts of the manuscript.

MULTINATIONALS, THE STATE, AND THE MANAGEMENT OF ECONOMIC NATIONALISM

1 MULTINATIONALS IN SMALL MINERAL-PRODUCING COUNTRIES

One of the characteristics of the international system that emerged after World War II has been the proliferation of multinational corporations (MNCs)[1] and their prominence as actors in the international arena. U.S.-based MNCs have enjoyed a clear dominance in the field, though Western European and Japanese firms have been closing in. In fact, Samuel P. Huntington has argued that U.S. business corporations and government-controlled transnational organizations have been the principal mechanisms of U.S. post-war expansion, creating an "American empire" characterized not by the acquisition of new territories but by the penetration of new territories. The dependence of Western Europe on the United States for protection against the Soviet Union in the immediate post-war period facilitated the entry of U.S. business corporations into these countries and into their colonies.[2]

The post-war international system has also seen a proliferation of nation states, as colonies of European powers acquired their political independence. With aspirations to industrialize and to modernize, many of these newly independent countries invited the MNCs in on very generous terms. A few attempted to extend their anti-colonial struggle against existing MNCs, particularly those in mining and in plantation agriculture. However, in the majority of the cases where MNCs were initially welcomed, the relations between the MNCs and the host governments have not been entirely harmonious.

The role of multinational corporations in developing countries has been the subject of great academic and general interest. Two sharply contrasting viewpoints exist concerning their contributions to the host country. The first sees the MNC in very benevolent terms. The MNC is seen as making enormous contributions to the host country's economy by providing employment, by contributing to government revenues through the payment of taxes, and by providing a ready export for the country. Further, the MNC is presented as the most promising instrument for the transfer of capital to the developing countries and as a transmission belt for the diffusion of technological and managerial skills to these countries. The second position is a direct negation of the first. In this view, the MNC has acquired a bad reputation for tax evasion, for stifling local enterprise by its sheer size and scope, and for failing in its promise to diffuse technological and managerial skills to the host country. Moreover, the MNC seems capable of wielding a tremendous amount of political influence within the host country and, by so doing, aggravates internal tensions and stimulates nationalism that is usually directed against the MNC.[3]

It is not surprising that the multinational corporation has been a central issue in the North-South conflict. The developing countries would like to impose an international code of conduct upon the MNCs, thereby acquiring for themselves some measure of control over these economic giants. So far, this goal has proved to be highly elusive and, at least in the short term, developing countries are constrained to seek ways of improving their position vis-à-vis the MNCs, within the present international framework.[4]

This study is concerned with the relations between mineral-producing Third World countries and MNCs involved in the extraction of these mineral resources. The principal focus, however, is on the small mineral producer[5] whose economy depends critically on its mineral-exporting sector. The study analyzes the opportunities available to a developing country with a limited mineral resource base, to improve its bargaining position with the MNCs involved in the extraction of its subsoil resources. Trinidad and Tobago[6] is used as an illustrative case study.

Trinidad is a small petroleum producer. The petroleum industry has always been dominated by multinationals. The study examines the opportunities and the means that have been available to the Trinidadian government to upgrade its bargaining position vis-à-vis the oil MNCs, within a domestic context in which the government also seeks to placate its supporters and to disarm its critics. The study utilizes a bargaining approach to examine the relationship between the Trinidadian government and the foreign investors in the oil industry over the period 1956 to 1985. It should be pointed out here that the same political party, the People's National Movement (PNM), controlled the government over the period covered by this study.

Trinidad is a particularly interesting case. Although the government of that country never committed itself to a program of nationalization, it did, in fact, nationalize several foreign enterprises, including oil companies. However, it did not nationalize the entire oil industry even when international conditions seemed propitious for such action and when domestic groups were clamoring for outright nationalization. Instead it chose nationalization only when all other options were foreclosed. It will be shown that this was the case in the government's acquisition of the Trinidadian assets of the following companies: British Petroleum, Shell, Tesoro, and Texaco.

The study will also show that the relationship between the PNM government and the oil multinationals went through two distinct phases. The first, which lasted from 1956 to 1969, saw the government playing the role of a passive tax collector. The second phase lasted from 1970 to 1985. During this period, the government pursued three goals simultaneously. It tried to maximize its share of the revenues from the oil industry and to appease domestic groups seeking the nationalization of the industry while simultaneously trying to induce the multinationals to remain in Trinidad.

The study will link the oil industry with certain developments in the sugar industry. The reason for this is that these two industries have traditionally been the principal pillars of the Trinidadian economy. They both have powerful domestic political constituencies. Groups seeking to push the multinationals out have attempted to link the two industries together, and, as this study will show, the sugar industry featured significantly in the efforts of the PNM government to blunt the drive for the nationalization of the oil industry.

THE CONCESSIONS PROCESS

Two perspectives dominate the literature on host-foreign investor relations: the dependency and the bargaining perspectives. In this section we will present the basic arguments of these respective schools as they relate to multinational corporations involved in mineral extraction in developing countries.

As Ronald H. Chilcote has pointed out, there is no unified theory of dependency. What is called dependency theory is, in fact, a variety of "theoretical tendencies," advanced to explain (Latin American) underdevelopment.[7] It is the Marxist tendency within dependency theory that gives greater attention to the MNCs.

André Gunder Frank, one of the earliest contributors to the Marxist school of dependency, saw the underdevelopment of the periphery rooted in the development of capitalism. According to Frank, the same historical process, namely, the development of capitalism, that generated the development of the "metropolitan" or center countries also generated the underdevelopment of the "satellite" or periphery countries. Frank saw foreign investment as an instrument for the extraction of capital from the underdeveloped satellites rather than as a mechanism for stimulating development. In fact, Frank predicted that when the markets for the agricultural or mineral commodities disappeared, the periphery countries would be abandoned to their own devices. Frank suggested that economic development in the satellite countries could occur only if the existing structure of metropolis-satellite relations were overthrown.[8] This presumably meant the nationalization of the multinationals.

Norman Girvan has applied the Frank thesis to mineral-exporting countries and, not surprisingly, has come up with essentially the same prescription. Girvan argues that the goals of multinationals operating in mineral-exporting countries are inconsistent with true economic development in those countries. The multinationals are interested in stabilizing production through diversification of sources and ultimately in profit maximization. For many developing nations exporting minerals, the minerals are their economic lifelines, and they would like to use the mineral industry as the basis for building a national economic system. Yet they are prevented from so doing because national economic decision-making in these countries is subordinate, not to national governments in the center countries, but to corporate boardrooms of multinational corporations located in the center countries. Girvan refers to this structure of domination as "corporate imperialism." Girvan sees the host government as the only entity that can stop the domination and exploitation. He advocates a strategy of economic liberation that would ultimately result in disengagement from the international capitalist system. Girvan sees nationalization of the multinationals also as a necessary, but not a sufficient condition for non-dependent growth.[9]

Nationalization of the multinationals has been endorsed by other dependency theorists. However, they have also cautioned against using this as the sole mechanism for ensuring economic growth in periphery countries. Immanuel Wallerstein, for instance, does not see nationalization of foreign enterprise in periphery and semi-periphery nations as altering the essence of the capitalist world economy. He argues that as long as these countries participate in the world market, nationalization of a foreign enterprise in any one of them merely creates a state-owned capitalist enterprise and the country remains a part of the capitalist world economy.[10]

Susanne Bodenheimer has criticized Frank's thesis for being unidimensional in the sense that it ignores other aspects of the metropolis-satellite relations such as the ideological hegemony of the dominant nations and of the local clientele elites. She argues that the international system also causes underdevelopment indirectly by creating and reinforcing an "infrastructure of dependency" within periphery countries. The infrastructure of dependency consists of certain institutions and social classes that serve the interests and needs of the center countries. She identifies these interests and needs as those of the center-based multinational corporations which she sees as the main units of imperialism. Bodenheimer argues that whereas it is necessary for periphery nations to nationalize foreign enterprise and to sever their ties with the international capitalist system, it is also important for them to engage in a socialist transformation of their own socioeconomic order in order to dismantle the internal infrastructure of dependency.[11]

To summarize, Marxist dependency writers propound the inevitability of conflict between the developing host country and the MNC. They see the MNC as the principal mechanism by which the advanced capitalist countries penetrate and exploit the economies of Third World countries. A direct result of this penetration is that the development of the Third World host countries becomes subordinate to the development of the advanced capitalist countries.

The dependency approach does not admit that bargaining of any importance occurs between the host country and the foreign investor. Negotiations between the host country and the foreign investor, insofar as these occur, dwell on marginal issues and do not usually address the crux of the problem, which is that the decision-making centers of the MNCs are located outside of the host country. As a consequence, decisions made in corporate boardrooms overseas seriously affect the host country but do not take into consideration the developmental priorities of the latter. The prescription that emerges from the dependency perspective is the nationalization of foreign enterprise by developing host countries as part of their overall effort to rupture the structure of dependency.

However, nationalizations are not occurring everywhere, and as Paul Sigmund points out in the context of Latin America, even in those countries in which nationalizations have taken place, an equilibrium position seems to have been reached that allows for the operations of foreign investors. This equilibrium position is a mixed economy and it seems to indicate that Latin American policymakers do not necessarily accept either the inevitability of conflict or the automatic harmony of interests upheld by advocates of free enterprise.[12] Because of this situation, the dependency approach is not very useful in shedding light on the interactions that continue to take place between developing host countries and foreign investors. It is not a useful predictor of the changes in the terms of exchange that take place between the two principal parties and that are the results of periodic renegotiations. Bargaining theory, as we will see, fulfills these functions more adequately.

Bargaining models may be divided into two groups: static bargaining models and dynamic bargaining models. Static bargaining models emphasize the initial negotiations that take place between the host government and the foreign investor, each of which exercises control over resources that the other needs, whereas dynamic models incorporate change over the life of the agreement.[13]

The model proposed by Robert L. Curry and Donald Rothchild fits the genre of a static bargaining model. Based on an examination of the experiences of African governments with multinational corporations, Curry and Rothchild propose a bargaining model in which "impatience" and "reciprocal demand intensity" are the key variables used to explain host government-MNC interactions. The authors argue that a prospective host country's impatience to conclude a deal with the MNC usually results in an arrangement in which the benefits to the government fall short of what they might have been if the negotiations had been more protracted. The authors do not explain the sources of the government's impatience. One is left with the impression that the government is impatient or it is not, and that the consequence of impatience is a contract that is unfavorable to the government. The second explanatory variable in the model is called "reciprocal demand intensity" and involves a comparison of the relative intensity between the state's desire for what the foreign firm has to offer and the firm's desire for what the state has to offer. In a particular bargain, the greater demand intensity on the part of the state arises from the absence of alternative firms, local or foreign, with which the state can negotiate. The final contract reflects the state's impatience for a deal as well as the relative intensity with which it desires the resources at the disposal of the MNC.[14]

The principal deficiency of the Curry-Rothchild model, as it applies to mineral-exporting economies, is that while it might explain some of the initial conditions surrounding the entry of the MNC into the developing country, it ignores the question of renegotiation of the original contract. The concession agreement is usually for an extended period of time, and as Smith and Wells point out, the initial negotiation of the contract is merely one step in a process of unfolding relationships. Smith and Wells suggest that the "concession contract" should be seen as part of a "concessions process" in which change is the principal characteristic.[15] Because Curry and Rothchild ignore the issue of renegotiation, they do not consider the impact of the host country's domestic politics on the bargaining process. Indeed, the model cannot explain why nationalization occurs in several mineral-exporting economies where concessional agreements for fairly extended periods are usually the norm. What is needed to better understand the various facets of renegotiation is an interactive bargaining model.

One such interactive bargaining model has been proposed by Raymond Mikesell. According to Mikesell, the strength of bargaining is initially on the side of the foreign investor and this is usually reflected in the terms of the concession agreement that is initially drawn up. The bargaining power of the foreign investor stems from the fact that the foreign investor can bring in the requisite capital, technology, management and organizational skills, and usually a world-wide marketing and distribution system. There is also a risk element involved. Before a shaft is sunk or a hole is drilled, there is no certainty that minerals actually exist beneath the surface. The host country is capital poor and is a risk-avoider. The foreign investor, on the other hand, is a risk-taker and the concession contract contains terms that reward the foreign investor for its risks.[16]

Real conflict between the host government and the foreign investor begins to emerge once the original concessionaire has established the existence and size of the mineral reserves and begins to develop the mineral on a commercial basis, thereby earning for itself a high return on its investment. The original risks are downplayed and the government or its political opposition might begin to feel that the original terms of the agreement were too generous and that the national resource is being given away. This sets the stage for renegotiation. The government's position is usually strengthened by burgeoning nationalism. As the foreign-controlled industry increases in visibility, that is, as it becomes more important in the national economy, it becomes the object of attack by domestic opposition forces.[17]

Developments in other countries also affect the bargaining positions of an MNC and its host. Developing countries compare the terms of their concession agreements with those recently negotiated in other countries or even in the same country. Even though the circumstances surrounding the other agreements might be different, strong pressures are generated in the host country for a renegotiation or updating of the terms of the original agreement.[18]

Mikesell also argues that as the developing host country grows in wealth and economic capability, there is a corresponding increase in its ability to take over and operate technically advanced enterprises. The fact that nationalization becomes a more feasible government option increases its bargaining power.[19]

The model elaborated by Mikesell emphasizes the economic aspects of bargaining between the foreign investor and the host government. It does not accurately reflect the impact of the domestic politics of the host country on the bargaining process. Domestic politics are an especially important factor in the relations between the host country and MNCs involved in a mineral-extracting industry. The removal of subsoil resources from the host country exposes the companies to charges of exploitation and provides domestic opposition groups with ample opportunity for nationalistic mobilization.

Theodore Moran has proposed what he considers to be a more dynamic model of host country-foreign investor relations. The model is based on an analysis of the experience of the foreign copper companies in Chile and is meant to account for the instability of concession agreements and, in particular, to explain why developing host countries nationalize foreign companies involved in the extraction of natural resources. Moran calls his model a balance-of-power model. It is, in fact, a bargaining model that concentrates on those developing countries with rich endowments of raw materials.

The model employs two explanatory variables: (i) uncertainty about whether the investment can be made a success; and (ii) a host-country learning curve. Moran argues that initially the preponderance of bargaining strength is on the side of the foreign investor. The starting position is one of monopoly control over the capacity to make a successful operation out of a potential ore-body. Since the host government cannot supply the capital or the technological and managerial services needed for the undertaking, and since it would like to see its natural resource become a source of revenue and employment, it must make the type of concessions that would be attractive to the foreign investor. If the venture is unsuccessful, other such ventures will require at least the same or greater inducements.[20]

However, if the venture is successful, a drastic change takes place in the foreign-host relationship. Old doubts are quickly forgotten and the host country can bring on pressure for renegotiation of the original terms of agreement. With proven reserves, the government can exact better terms from other companies seeking to invest there, and it can use these terms to pressure the original concessionaire to revise its agreement in line with the newer agreements. Therefore, once the uncertainty has been reduced, bargaining power shifts from the foreign investor to the host government. On this point, Moran is in agreement with Mikesell and others.[21]

Moran argues further that successful ventures of this type would now provide an incentive for the host country to develop the skills and expertise appropriate to the industry, because it stands to increase its benefits by so doing. However, as the host country moves up the "learning curve" of negotiating skills and of direct operating skills for the industry, there is a transfer of power from the foreign investor to the host country, or, put differently, the balance of power shifts in favor of the host country. This shift in bargaining power is not oscillatory but cumulative; that is, as the host country acquires more knowledge about the operations of that natural resource industry, there is a cumulative shift in power away from the foreign investor to the host country. A point will be reached when the host country has developed the ability to replicate the functions of the foreign investor and the burden falls on the foreign investor to demonstrate what advantages its continued presence offers. National ownership now becomes a possibility.[22]

Moran differentiates between short-run shifts in the balance of power and a cumulative shift in the balance of power. He attributes short-run shifts to changes in the perception of uncertainty and cumulative shifts to the national learning process, that is, the domestic acquisition of skills and confidence appropriate to the industry.[23]

In Moran's model, economic nationalism[24] plays a significant role. In the case of Chile, it began as a struggle against *dependencia*, a term that was never clearly defined, but that presumably evoked strong emotional reaction and served as a source of inspiration for the development of the technological and managerial competence to bring the foreign corporations under national control. As the host country moved up the learning curve, that is, as its confidence increased, economic nationalism increased. Economic nationalism was also an outgrowth of domestic politics. Domestic political parties tried to win support by attacking the foreign companies. Eventually, the Chilean government nationalized the foreign copper companies when it felt that the country had the domestic competence to run the copper industry and when other impetuses to economic nationalism demanded such a course of action.

Like Moran, Franklin Tugwell agrees that the relationship between the host country and the MNC involved in the extractive sector is unstable and degenerates over time. Based on the experience of the foreign oil companies in Venezuela, however, Tugwell argues that the "degenerative instability" of concession agreements is only partly explained by the shift in bargaining power to the host government, as the MNCs sink more and more capital into the industry and thereby become vulnerable to pressures for renegotiation. However, the main source of this instability is the mistrust and uncertainty that are built into the concessionary system. The host country is never comfortable with the profit calculations of the foreign companies and is constantly in doubt about whether company decision-makers outside of the country might not be employing a variety of mechanisms to punish the host country for its assertiveness in seeking to maximize its income. On the other hand, the companies grow insecure about the longevity of any agreement with the host country. The insecurity on the part of the MNCs accounts for their attempts to influence public policy by manipulating economic variables such as production rates, prices, and reinvestment, by playing producer countries off against each other, and also by intervening directly in the domestic political process of the host country. In the short term, the MNCs often get their way. But in the long run, governmental and other domestic leaders learn that the corporations cannot be trusted and must be controlled.[25]

Both Moran and Tugwell have dealt with large natural resource-producing countries. Both predict nationalization of the foreign enterprise as the eventual outcome of the bargaining process between the host government and the foreign investor. However, as we will show in this study, the incentive structure for small mineral-producing countries is different from that of major resource producers and nationalization of the foreign investor cannot as easily be predicted. Bargaining power is not cumulative but oscillatory, and in this regard, the Mikesell model has greater applicability than those of Moran and Tugwell.

Although the emphasis varies among them, most writers on the bargaining approach to host country-MNC relations acknowledge that economic nationalism is a factor that must be taken into account. There does seem to be general agreement that expressions of nationalism by domestic groups strengthen the host government's bargaining position. Moran and Tugwell subscribe to this view. Both emphasize the intersection of state-MNC bargaining and the domestic politics of the host country. Both explain how the MNC directly or indirectly inspires economic nationalism and how the host government can capitalize on this to nationalize the MNC.

There are other contributors to the literature on MNCs, however, who alert us to the possibility that economic nationalism could interfere with the host government's development goals and could invite attempts by the government to control or manage it. Sylvia Ann Hewlett, for instance, has argued, with reference to Brazil, that the willingness to subdue labor is part of the price that a late developing country must pay in order to achieve industrial take-off.[26] And Kenneth Mericle has described specific controls that the Brazilian government has imposed on labor in that country.[27] Of course, the principal beneficiaries of greater state control over the more militant domestic groups are the foreign investor and the government.

Girvan also sees labor as one of the principal agents of economic nationalism in mineral-exporting countries. He argues that in its attempt to increase and stabilize its revenues from the MNC, the government will use repressive measures against labor.[28] Yet the Moran and Tugwell studies show that this was not the case in large mineral-producing countries.

The present study examines how the government of one small mineral-producing country responded to economic nationalism. Specifically, it shows how the intersection of domestic political considerations and sensitivity to national dependence on mineral resources shaped a government's response to demands for the nationalization of foreign-based mineral-extracting companies.

THE CASE OF THE SMALL MINERAL-PRODUCING COUNTRY

In this section, the key parameters circumscribing the bargaining position of small mineral producers are examined. The essential argument is that the bargaining position of a state dependent on small mineral reserves is markedly different from that of one with larger reserves, and the ability of such a state to effectively deal with the MNCs depends on its ability to manage its domestic politics.

An important factor in the bargaining process is the attractiveness of the particular raw material as an investment opportunity. The value of a mineral is a function of its scarcity, the quality of the ore or crude oil, and the comparative costs of developing the source. However, it is also a function of the essentiality of the commodity to the advanced industrialized countries.

Essentiality is an assessment of the relative significance of a raw material to a nation's security and to its economic well-being and is a measure of the damage or the dislocation that can be caused by a prolonged disruption of supplies of that commodity.[29] Since the industrialized countries provide the primary market for Third World raw materials, essentiality of a commodity features in the company's assessment of the profitability of investing in its production.

Ruth and Uzi Arad have come up with a ranking of raw materials based on essentiality (Table 1.1). From the company's point of view, investment in a commodity further up in the hierarchy would be more lucrative than one lower down. Host-country bargaining strategies are also affected by the commodity in question. In the case of a small producer, the essentiality of the commodity could very well dictate whether a marginal source is developed or not. In short, a country with a small reserve of petroleum or copper or iron ore stands a better chance of attracting a foreign investor to develop its resource than a country with a small reserve of tin.

Table 1.1   Priorities of Materials (on a scale of 1 to 10)

(1) RANK	(2) NAME OF MATERIAL	(3) DIFFICULTY OF SUBSTITUTION	(4) ECONOMIC IMPORTANCE	(5) INDUSTRIAL LEVERAGE	(6) GEOMETRIC MEAN OF COLUMNS 3-5
1	Iron Ore	8	10	9	8.96
2	Petroleum	8	9	8	8.32
3	Copper	6	6	5	6.32
4	Aluminum	6	6	5	5.65
5	Manganese	7	1	8	3.83
6	Nickel	4	2	4	3.17
7	Silver	8	1	4	3.17
8	Cobalt	7	1	4	3.04
9	Chromium	5	1	5	2.92
10	Platinum	8	1	3	2.88
11	Lead	5	1	4	2.71
12	Uranium	2	1	9	2.62
13	Mercury	7	1	2	2.41
14	Tin	3	1	3	2.08
15	Zinc	2	1	4	2.00

Source: Reproduced from Ruth W. Arad and Uzi B. Arad, Sharing Global Resources (New York: McGraw-Hill Book Company, 1979), p. 51.

As in the case of larger producers, the initial bargaining position of the small producer is weak. While the host government needs the revenues that could be generated from minerals believed to exist beneath the surface, it lacks the technology, capital, and managerial expertise to establish the size of its resources and to exploit these resources. Unlike countries with large proven reserves, however, a small mineral-producing country cannot easily downplay the element of risk in the foreign investor's operations, even after commercial production begins. The host country's hopes for an expansion of its reserves depend on the continuation of exploration activities by the foreign company, which is usually in possession of all of the seismic data. Opportunities exist, therefore, for the foreign investor to manipulate the continued existence of risk in its operations in order to keep the host country's bargaining position weak.

Widespread knowledge of the smallness of the reserves adversely affects the reservoir of local expertise that would develop around that commodity. People would be little inclined to commit careers in an area of economic activity perceived to be of short duration. Even if one were to discount the problem of attracting trainable skills, then, operating on the Moran thesis, the rate of development of technological and managerial expertise must keep sufficiently ahead of the rate of depletion of the resource if the expertise is to impact favorably on the bargaining position of the host government. And in the case of the small producer, where there is no reason for the foreign investor to practice conservation, the time span is too short for an indigenous work force to acquire the sophisticated skills necessary to run the enterprise.

It follows, therefore, that the host country's initial dependence on the foreign investor's technological, managerial, and marketing expertise is likely to be maintained for the duration of the concession agreement and that nationalization of the foreign investor is not a feasible option. This suggests that the Moran thesis is not applicable to the small producer; that is, the "learning curve" of technological and managerial skills is not a useful predictor of shifts in bargaining strength between the foreign investor and the host government.

Nationalization as a host-government option is also deterred by the cost of compensation as compared with the expected flow of profits from the industry under conditions of local ownership and management; by developmental pressures and the need for a steady stream of revenues from the mineral industry; and by the vulnerability of the host government to sanctions from the foreign investor's home country, as well as from the international investing community. As Paul Sigmund points out, the principle that some compensation must be paid in the event of nationalization has been recognized even by countries whose official ideology opposes private ownership of the means of production.[30]

The cost of compensation is usually very high and would pose a strain to many developing countries. Not only must capital be diverted from other national development projects, but revenues generated by the nationalized industry can be expected to fall. State ownership runs the risk of a decline in efficiency in the general management of the industry. Managerial appointments might involve political as opposed to strictly business considerations. Labor unions might accelerate their demands for wage increases which the government would find politically difficult to deny. The state-run industry can expect to face marketing difficulties. It may lose the traditional customers and marketing channels of the multinational corporation. It would have to develop a certain degree of marketing expertise relevant to the commodity. It would then be competing with experienced multinationals for markets in the developed countries. Lack of knowledge of the markets and the smallness of its exports relative to other producers would prove to be severe handicaps. The ability of the government to diversify the destinations of its export or simply to shift out of a particular market would be impaired by the smallness of its supply. The country might simply become a supplier of last resort. These considerations would militate against a strategy of nationalization. Even if nationalization is contemplated by the host government, its consummation might be forestalled by resistance on the part of the MNCs, frequently with the support of their home governments, and also by the host government's fears of the damage nationalization would do to the country's image as an attractive investment site.

The same factors which proscribe nationalization as an effective strategy for the host country greatly strengthen the bargaining position of the MNC. The MNC enters the host country with the knowledge that its stay there will be relatively brief as compared with its investments elsewhere. Uprooting in the short term has, therefore, already entered the investment calculus. This gives the MNC a bargaining ace and imposes an upper penalty on the bargaining position of the host country: The MNC can threaten to uproot whenever it decides that the host government's claims are excessive. In other words, the threat by the MNC to uproot in the short term is more potent against the small mineral-producing country than it is against a major producer, and it substantially enhances the MNC's bargaining position vis-à-vis the former.

This is not to say that the host government is not under pressure, and does not, in fact, try to renegotiate the terms of the agreement. Pressures on the government for renegotiation usually arise from (i) the need for revenues to achieve developmental goals; (ii) the need to assuage domestic groups such as labor and opposition parties; and (iii) external factors, primarily increases in the price of the commodity on the world market. However, pressures for a renegotiation can also arise from the MNC in circumstances such as a drop in the world market price of the commodity or unexpected increases in the cost of production. Thus the bargaining between the host government and the MNC is fairly fluid, especially since nationalization is not a credible option for the small mineral producer.

In its bargaining with the multinational corporation, the host government of a small mineral-producing country is motivated by two principal goals: to try to increase its share of the revenues generated by mineral industry; and to keep the multinational operating in the country. When the pickings are good, the government must be strong enough to press its claims for a greater share. When the going is rough, the state must be prepared to provide the MNC with inducements to remain and produce. In short, for the duration of the investment, there is always a quest for a win-win solution. This, of course, requires a host government with a great degree of flexibility.

As the foreign-controlled industry increases in importance to the economy, that is, as the size of its contribution to the economy increases, it will become more and more of an issue of domestic politics. The ability of the host government to achieve its principal goals would depend on its ability to manage its domestic politics. In a large mineral-producing country, the existence of a radical opposition party or of vocal nationalistic groups, demanding greater state control over the industry, strengthens the bargaining position of the host government. The MNC's intransigence in its bargaining with the host government could contribute to the opposition party riding a nationalistic wave into government and probably nationalizing the enterprise. The loss of a major mineral concession would be considerable to the MNC. Hence, the MNC is more likely to make concessions. In the case of a small mineral-producing country, however, the existence of a radical opposition party or of vocal nationalistic groups only marginally strengthens the bargaining position of the host government since voluntary relinquishment of this mineral resource would not severely jeopardize the MNC's global position. Since an early departure was envisioned anyway, due to the small size of the reserves, all that would happen is that this departure would be accelerated when the MNC views the host country's demands as excessive. The greater loser would be the government. The government is usually aware of this and must manage economic nationalism within the country so that it does not scare away the MNCs.

THEORETICAL SIGNIFICANCE OF THE STUDY

The literature on the dynamic relationship between extractive multinational corporations and developing host countries draws heavily on case studies of large natural resource-producing countries. Yet the conclusions reached about host-MNC relations in such settings are not entirely generalizable to small resource-producing countries. This case study of Trinidad, a small petroleum producer, is an attempt to remedy the omission in the literature.

There are numerous small producers of mineral resources. Take the case of petroleum, for instance. In 1980, The World in Figures listed 61 countries as the main producers of crude oil. Forty-five of these countries had production figures in 1976 that were smaller than 1 percent of the total world production. Of these, 28 were developing countries, and in 13 of these countries, petroleum and petroleum products accounted for over 20 percent of total exports. In the case of 8 of the developing countries, petroleum and petroleum products accounted for over 50 percent of their total exports for that year.[31] From the point of view of these countries, this commodity is essential to their economic well-being. How these nation-states deal with the MNCs involved in the development of their resources is an important question. The MNCs are crucial to the achievement of development goals in these countries. The MNCs are one of the principal means by which economically marginal states are integrated into the international system. The questions that are pursued in this study allow us to understand better some of what Robert Keohane refers to as the Lilliputians' dilemmas.[32]

NOTES

1. As used in this study, a multinational corporation is a company with its parent headquarters in one country and subsidiary operations in at least one other country. See Ronald Muller, "The Multinational Corporation and the Underdevelopment of the Third World," in Charles K. Wilber, ed., The Political Economy of Development and Underdevelopment (New York: Random House, 1979), p. 151.

2. Samuel P. Huntington, "Transnational Organizations in World Politics," World Politics 25 (April 1973), pp. 342-347.

3. For a summary of the positions of the two schools, see John Diebold, "Multinational Corporations. . . Why Be Scared of Them?" Foreign Policy 12 (Fall 1973), pp. 84-85. For a defense of the multinationals, see Orville Freeman, The Multinational Company: Instrument for World Growth (New York: Praeger Publishers, 1981). For a contrasting viewpoint, see Richard J. Barnet and Ronald E. Muller, Global Reach: The Power of the Multinational Corporations (New York: Simon and Schuster, 1974).

4. Some of the proposals for new economic order are discussed in Jagdish N. Bhagwati, ed., The New International Economic Order: The North-South Debate (Cambridge, Mass.: M.I.T. Press, 1977).

5. In this study, a small mineral-producing country is defined as one whose annual production of the mineral is less than 1 percent of total world production.

6. Hereafter referred to simply as Trinidad.

7. Ronald H. Chilcote, "A Question of Dependency," Latin American Research Review 13 (1978), p. 55.

8. André Gunder Frank, "The Development of Underdevelopment," in James D. Cockcroft, André Gunder Frank, and Dale L. Johnson, Dependence and Underdevelopment: Latin America's Political Economy (New York: Anchor Books, 1972), pp. 3-17.

9. Norman Girvan, Corporate Imperialism: Conflict and Expropriation (White Plains, New York: M. E. Sharpe, Inc., 1976), pp. 3-51, 188-199.

10. Although Wallerstein may not be a dependentista, his world-system theory draws heavily from dependency theory. See Immanuel Wallerstein, The Capitalist World-Economy (Cambridge: Cambridge University Press, 1979), pp. 66-92. See also Daniel Chirot and Thomas D. Hall, "World-System Theory," Annual Review of Sociology 8 (1982), pp. 90-93.

11. Susanne Bodenheimer, "Dependency and Imperialism: The Roots of Latin American Underdevelopment," Politics and Society 1 (May 1971), pp. 335-355.

12. Paul E. Sigmund, Multinationals in Latin America: The Politics of Nationalization (Madison: The University of Wisconsin Press, 1980), pp. 278-279.

13. David N. Smith and Louis T. Wells, Jr., Negotiating Third-World Mineral Agreements: Promises as Prologue (Cambridge, Mass.: Ballinger Publishing Company, 1975), pp. 4-5.

14. Robert L. Curry, Jr. and Donald Rothchild, "On Economic Bargaining between African Governments and Multinational Companies," The Journal of Modern African Studies 12 (February 1974), pp. 173-182.

15. Smith and Wells, Jr., Negotiating Third-World Mineral Agreements, p. 3.

16. Raymond F. Mikesell, "Conflict in Foreign Investor-Host Country Relations: A Preliminary Analysis," in Raymond F. Mikesell, ed., Foreign Investment in the Petroleum and Mineral Industries: Case Studies of Investor-Host Country Relations (Baltimore: The Johns Hopkins Press, 1971), p. 38.

17. Ibid., p. 39.

18. Ibid., p. 39.

19. Ibid., p. 39.

20. Theodore H. Moran, Multinational Corporations and the Politics of Dependence: Copper in Chile (Princeton: Princeton University Press, 1974), pp. 159-160.

21. Ibid., pp. 160-161. See also Smith and Wells, Jr., Negotiating Third-World Mineral Agreements, pp. 18-19.

22. Moran, Multinational Corporations, pp. 162-166.

23. Ibid., pp. 166-169.

24. Although Moran does not explicitly define the term economic nationalism, the definition inferred from his discussion of *dependencia* and used in the present study may be stated thus: Economic nationalism in a developing country is a domestic reaction against foreign influence in the political and economic life of the country. It manifests itself in the country's domestic desire to reassert sovereign control over its affairs. See Moran, Multinational Corporations, pp. 3-15.

25. Franklin Tugwell, The Politics of Oil in Venezuela (Stanford: Stanford University Press, 1975), pp. 145-175.

26. For an examination of the developmental dilemmas confronting a late developing country, see Sylvia Ann Hewlett, The Cruel Dilemmas of Development: Twentieth Century Brazil (New York: Basic Books, 1980).

27. Kenneth S. Mericle, "Corporatist Control of the Working Class: Authoritarian Brazil since 1964," in James M. Malloy, ed., Authoritarianism and Corporatism in Latin America (Pittsburgh: University of Pittsburgh Press, 1977), pp. 303-334.

28. Norman Girvan, Corporate Imperialism, pp. 36-40.

29. Ruth W. Arad and Uzi B. Arad, Sharing Global Resources (New York: McGraw-Hill Book Company, 1979), pp. 48-51.

30. Sigmund, Multinationals in Latin America, pp. 265-266.

31. The Economist, The World in Figures (New York: Facts on File, Inc., 1980), pp. 29-31.

32. Robert Keohane, "Lilliputians' Dilemmas: Small States in International Politics," International Organization 23 (Spring 1969), pp. 291-311.

2 AN OPEN
PETROLEUM
ECONOMY

The two-island state of Trinidad and Tobago has an area of about 2000 square miles and is situated on the continental shelf close to Venezuela. Trinidad was sighted by Columbus in 1498 and was named in honor of the Holy Trinity. The island experienced three centuries of Spanish rule before it was captured by the British. Tobago historically enjoyed greater strategic importance than Trinidad and changed hands among European powers before finally remaining under British control after 1803. In 1889, Tobago was linked to Trinidad for easier administration and the town of Port-of-Spain served as the administrative center. Trinidad and Tobago was a member of the short-lived Federation of the West Indies (1958-1962), but withdrew after Jamaica did so in 1961. The country became independent of Britain on August 31, 1962, and became a republic in 1975.[1]

The national government of Trinidad is organized as a parliamentary democracy. Parliament is bicameral: The House of Representatives consists of 36 elected members, and the Senate consists of 31 seats, which are divided among the political parties in direct proportion to the number of elected seats that each wins in the House of Representatives. National elections for the House of Representatives are held every five years. The titular head of state is the president, who is elected by both Houses of Parliament. However, the actual locus of power resides in the position of the prime minister, who heads the cabinet and is selected from the party that commands the support of the majority of the members of the House of Representatives.

Trinidad is the most prosperous of the independent countries of the Caribbean. In 1984, the per capita gross national product (GNP) of Trinidad was 7150 U.S. dollars. This was the second highest of all the middle-income countries of the world and the highest in Latin America.[2] Table 2.1 shows how Trinidad compares with some selected countries on a few basic

Table 2.1   Comparison of Trinidad with Selected Countries
on Some Socioeconomic Indicators

COUNTRY	GNP PER CAPITA (U.S. dollars) 1984	AVERAGE ANNUAL GROWTH (%) 1965-1984	ADULT LITERACY RATE (%)	LIFE EXPECTANCY AT BIRTH (yrs) 1984
Trinidad	7,150	2.6	95	69
United States	15,390	1.7	99	76
United Kingdom	8,570	1.6	99	74
Singapore	7,260	7.8	83	72
Hong Kong	6,330	6.2	90	76
Venezuela	3,410	0.9	82	69
Brazil	1,720	4.6	76	64
Costa Rica	1,190	1.6	90	73
Jamaica	1,150	0.4	90	73

Source: The World Bank, World Development Report, 1986 (New York: Oxford
University Press, 1986). Adult literacy rates from the World Bank, World Tables,
Volume II (Baltimore: The Johns Hopkins University Press, 1984).

socioeconomic indicators.   International lending agencies have ceased ranking Trinidad as a developing country.[3]   However, although it possesses some
of the characteristics of a developed country--notably, a relatively high per
capita GNP, a high literacy rate, and a high life expectancy at birth--Trinidad
remains, as will become clear in this study, a developing country.   Its relative
prosperity is accounted for by its petroleum industry.

CONTRIBUTION OF THE PETROLEUM SECTOR

Trinidad is an open petroleum economy.[4]   The performance of the
economy mainly reflects developments in the petroleum sector, which in turn
is affected by conditions in the world market for petroleum.   There is no
question that, at least until 1982, Trinidad was a grateful beneficiary of the
international petroleum price regime put in place by the OPEC cartel.
Thereafter, the Trinidadian economy began to contract, again reflecting
trends in the international petroleum economy.

Table 2.2 shows the gross domestic product (GDP) at current factor
cost over the period 1960 to 1985.   The gross domestic product peaked in
1982.   In that year, the GDP was over six times what it was in 1973, showing
the enormous expansion of the economy as a result of the OPEC price
regime.   Table 2.3 shows the GDP at constant factor cost over the period

Table 2.2   Gross Domestic Product (GDP) at Current Factor Cost,
1960-1985 (millions of U.S. dollars)

YEAR	GDP	EXCHANGE RATE ANNUAL AVERAGE (T. T. dollars per U.S. dollar)
1960	466.4	1.71
1961	512.6	1.71
1962	541.6	1.71
1963	579.5	1.71
1964	605.3	1.71
1965	660.6	1.71
1966	729.6	1.71
1967	771.8	1.74
1968	761.9	2.00
1969	781.1	2.00
1970	829.9	2.00
1971	907.0	1.98
1972	1,079.0	1.92
1973	1,316.0	1.96
1974	2,015.7	2.05
1975	2,418.2	2.17
1976	2,493.3	2.44
1977	3,125.3	2.40
1978	3,557.9	2.40
1979	4,702.7	2.40
1980	6,299.5	2.40
1981	6,971.5	2.40
1982	8,346.5	2.40
1983	7,969.9	2.40
1984	7,941.0	2.40
1985	7,411.1	2.45

Source: Figures for 1960-1981 were compiled from the World Bank, World Tables, Volume I (1976, 1980, 1983).   Figures   for 1982-1985 were obtained from the Republic of Trinidad and Tobago, Review of the Economy 1984 and Review of the Economy 1986. Exchange rates for 1982-1985 were provided by the Federal Reserve Bank, Atlanta, Georgia.   All financial figures have been converted from T.T. dollars to U.S. dollars.

1960 to 1985. The average annual rate of growth in real terms over the period 1960 to 1981 was an impressive 5.0 percent, with the highest growth rates occurring over the period of 1976 to 1981 when the average annual growth rate was 7.1 percent. However, after 1982, there was a serious contraction of the Trinidadian economy, reflecting adverse trends in the international petroleum economy. The average annual real rate of growth over the period 1982 to 1985 was minus 5.7 percent.

Table 2.4 shows the contribution of the petroleum sector to the GDP at current factor cost. Over the period of 1960 to 1973, the average annual percentage contribution of the petroleum sector to GDP at factor cost was approximately 27 percent. However, over the period 1974 to 1985, under the prevailing OPEC price regime, the petroleum sector's contribution to GDP averaged 37.7 percent annually. In several years within this period, the petroleum sector's contribution to GDP exceeded 40 percent.

Petroleum and petroleum products account for the greater proportion of domestic exports (Table 2.5). Over the period 1962 to 1983, these products accounted for an average of 84.4 percent annually. Between 1974 and 1983, the contribution of the industry to total exports averaged 89.1 percent annually. When the export figures are disaggregated to reflect the separate contributions of crude oil and refinery products, we find that Trinidad has been much more important as a refining center than as an exporter of crude oil. As column 3 of Table 2.5 shows, between 1962 and 1973, crude oil exports averaged 8.7 percent of total exports annually. However, over the same period, refinery products accounted for an average of 71.7 percent of total exports annually (column 5). With the quadrupling of crude oil prices after 1973, the crude oil proportion of total annual exports increased markedly but, as a comparison between columns 3 and 5 of Table 2.5 shows, the contribution of refinery products to total exports has been consistently higher than that of crude oil. The bulk of the crude oil refined in Trinidad was brought into the country by Texaco, which also marketed the end products. As a result the country became very dependent on Texaco (see Chapter 3).

A final indicator of the petroleum sector's dominant role in the economy is the contribution of this sector to government revenues. As Table 2.6 shows, between 1972 and 1985, the petroleum sector's contribution to total government revenues averaged 48 percent annually. However, between 1974 and 1981, the period that oil prices were highest, the petroleum sector's contribution to government revenues averaged about 62 percent annually. Thus the petroleum sector has, without a doubt, been the "golden goose" of the Trinidadian economy.

STATE CONTRIBUTION TO COMMERCIAL ENTERPRISES

Expanding state revenues, particularly after 1973, have given rise to other types of dependencies on the oil sector. This can be seen in the expanding public sector activities. In 1977, the government had an equity interest in 50 companies. Twenty-three of these companies were wholly owned by the government, which held a majority interest in 13 others and a

Table 2.3   Gross Domestic Product (GDP) at Constant Factor Cost
(1970 prices), 1960-1985

YEAR	GDP AT CONSTANT FACTOR COST (millions of U.S. dollars)	ANNUAL REAL GROWTH RATE PERCENT
1960	532.7	
1961	579.6	8.8
1962	595.0	2.7
1963	613.2	3.1
1964	635.2	3.6
1965	684.4	7.7
1966	727.1	6.2
1967	751.3	3.3
1968	773.2	2.9
1969	790.1	2.2
1970	829.9	5.0
1971	848.3	2.2
1972	887.4	4.6
1973	933.0	5.1
1974	957.0	2.6
1975	961.5	0.0
1976	1,052.2	9.4
1977	1,133.6	7.7
1978	1,219.4	7.6
1979	1,308.2	7.3
1980	1,397.0	6.8
1981	1,496.6	7.1
1982	1,490.8	0.0
1983	1,385.6	-7.1
1984	1,208.4	-12.8
1985	1,173.0	-2.9

Source: GDP figures for 1960-1981 were compiled from the World Bank, World Tables, Volume I,   (1976, 1980, 1983). GDP figures for 1982-1985 were obtained from the Republic of Trinidad and   Tobago, Review of the Economy 1984 and Review of the Economy 1986. Where necessary, figures were deflated to reflect 1970 prices. All financial figures were converted from T.T. dollars to U.S. dollars.

Table 2.4   Contribution of the Petroleum Sector to
GDP at Current Factor Cost, 1960-1985

YEAR	GDP AT CURRENT FACTOR COST (millions of U.S. dollars)	PETROLEUM SECTOR (millions of U.S. dollars)	PETROLEUM SECTOR AS A PERCENTAGE OF GDP AT CURRENT FACTOR COST
1960	466.4	154.0	33.0
1961	512.6	167.1	32.6
1962	541.6	170.5	31.5
1963	579.5	171.2	29.5
1964	605.3	176.0	29.1
1965	660.6	166.1	25.2
1966	729.6	189.8	26.0
1967	771.8	208.5	27.0
1968	761.9	221.9	29.1
1969	781.1	192.7	24.6
1970	829.9	180.6	21.8
1971	907.0	183.7	20.3
1972	1,079.0	220.4	20.4
1973	1,316.0	359.7	27.5
1974	2,015.7	897.4	44.5
1975	2,418.2	1,215.2	50.3
1976	2,493.5	1,216.1	48.8
1977	3,125.3	1,519.6	48.6
1978	3,557.9	1,486.7	41.8
1979	4,702.7	1,697.0	36.1
1980	6,299.5	2,687.3	42.7
1981	6,971.5	2,625.8	37.7
1982	8,346.5	2,254.6	27.0
1983	7,969.9	1,935.7	24.3
1984	7,941.0	2,043.8	25.7
1985	7,411.1	1,814.7	24.5

Source: Contributions of the petroleum sector to GDP for the years 1960-1974 were
compiled from the Central Statistical Office, Annual Statistical Abstract (1962-
1976). Figures for 1975-1981 were compiled from the Republic of Trinidad and
Tobago, Review of the Economy (1979, 1981, and 1982). Figures for 1982-1985
were obtained from the Central Statistical Office, Annual Statistical Abstract 1985.
All financial figures have been converted from T.T. dollars to U.S. dollars.

minority interest in the remaining 14.[5] These companies, particularly those that are completely state-owned, operate without the external discipline of the market and with varying degrees of profitability and yet continue to have access to government funds. Take the case of the sugar industry, for instance. In 1975, the government nationalized the foreign-owned sugar companies. Since 1976, the industry has been suffering severe losses and requires an annual bail-out by the government. Despite the performance of the industry, wages in the industry continue to rise rapidly. For example, in 1976, wage rates for manual workers in the industry rose to about twice what they were in 1973,[6] despite the fact that the industry incurred a loss in 1976 of about eight to nine million dollars (U.S.).[7] This situation is not peculiar to the sugar industry. The state-owned airline, British West Indian Airways (BWIA), is nationally known to be a money-loser, as is the Iron and Steel Company of Trinidad and Tobago (ISCOTT).

Table 2.7 shows the amount the PNM government contributed over the period 1973 to 1983 to companies in which the government has an equity interest. On an annual basis, the government has contributed an average of about 15 percent of its total revenue to the support of these industries. From a low of US$15.9 million in 1973, the government's contribution to commercial enterprises reached a high of US$609 million in 1982. This represented an increase of over 3700 percent. The government's ability to continue this sizable support for these commercial enterprises stemmed largely from the huge revenues coming in from the petroleum sector. However, poor performance of these enterprises inspired strong public opposition to further expansion of the state sector. It is interesting to note that the National Alliance for Reconstruction (NAR), which replaced the PNM in government in 1986, promised to privatize the economy.

EMPLOYMENT AND GENERAL WELFARE

Although revenues from the oil industry have made the country financially secure, the problem of unemployment still remains. The oil industry is highly capital-intensive and therefore provides employment for only a few people. In 1981, for example, out of a total labor force of 431,400, the oil industry provided employment to about 19,333 people, or about 4.5 percent of the labor force.[8] It becomes a burden on the other sectors of the economy to absorb the rest of the labor force. This has been done largely through the agricultural, the public service, the construction, and the services sectors.

The government of Trinidad is the largest employer of labor in the country. In 1981, administrative, professional, technical, clerical, and manual workers in the public service accounted for a total of about 94,500 people, or about 22 percent of the total labor force.[9] However, this did not include the people employed in the government's "special works" program. This program is organized under the Development and Environmental Works Division (DEWD) and employs people on a rotating basis, usually guaranteeing work for only two weeks at a time. They are supposed to be employed in beautifying the country but in practice do little work. Although the

Table 2.5   Export of Petroleum and Petroleum Products, 1962-1983

Year	(1) Value of Total Exports ($1,000 U.S.)	(2) Exports of Crude Oil ($1,000 U.S.)	(3) (2) as % of (1)	(4) Exports of Petroleum Products ($1,000 U.S.)	(5) (4) as % of (1)	(6) (2) + (4) ($1,000 U.S.)	(7) (2) + (4) as % of (1)
1962	338,115	19,605	5.8	268,750	79.5	288,355	85.3
1963	364,339	21,535	5.9	285,100	78.3	306,635	84.2
1964	400,290	29,387	7.3	305,375	76.3	334,762	83.6
1965	395,658	29,853	7.5	298,731	75.5	328,584	83.0
1966	418,325	31,335	7.5	307,533	73.5	338,868	81.0
1967	433,642	37,794	8.7	306,262	70.6	344,056	79.3
1968	466,251	38,358	8.2	323,871	69.5	362,229	77.7
1969	474,584	43,116	9.1	322,338	67.9	365,454	77.0
1970	481,526	37,038	7.7	334,307	69.4	371,335	78.2
1971	520,450	39,068	7.5	363,142	69.8	402,209	77.3
1972	557,637	55,152	9.9	377,762	67.7	432,914	77.6
1973	695,745	135,964	19.5	435,555	62.6	571,519	82.1
1974	2,037,665	597,245	29.3	1,238,429	60.8	1,835,674	90.1
1975	1,772,728	660,413	37.3	881,261	49.7	1,541,674	87.0
1976	2,219,267	747,010	33.7	1,257,712	56.7	2,004,723	90.3
1977	2,179,814	856,575	39.3	1,138,142	52.2	1,994,716	91.5
1978	2,042,713	847,926	41.5	977,539	47.9	1,825,465	89.4
1979	2,610,436	985,308	37.7	1,376,570	52.7	2,361,878	90.5
1980	4,077,017	1,635,292	40.1	2,131,727	52.3	3,767,019	92.4
1981	3,760,821	1,612,356	42.9	1,741,636	46.3	3,353,992	89.2
1982	3,085,453	1,116,363	36.2	1,583,156	51.3	2,699,519	87.5
1983	2,352,664	1,099,437	46.7	858,521	36.5	1,957,958	83.2

Source: Compiled from the United Nations, <u>Yearbook of International Trade Statistics</u> (New York: The United Nations, 1965-1984).

Table 2.6   Central Government Revenues, 1972-1985
(millions of U.S. dollars)

YEAR	OIL SECTOR REVENUES	NON-OIL SECTOR REVENUES	TOTAL GOVERNMENT REVENUES	OIL SECTOR REVENUES AS A PERCENTAGE OF TOTAL
1972	41.2	176.4	217.6	18.9
1973	59.3	193.7	253.0	23.4
1974	470.0	205.9	875.9	69.5
1975	592.8	259.1	851.9	69.6
1976	576.3	368.7	945.0	61.0
1977	748.9	497.4	1,246.3	60.0
1978	712.8	589.8	1,302.6	54.7
1979	984.4	707.2	1,691.6	58.2
1980	1,733.5	973.1	2,706.6	64.0
1981	1,828.8	1,085.6	2,914.4	62.8
1982	1,126.8	1,839.0	2,965.8	40.0
1983	824.7	1,910.1	2,734.8	30.2
1984	906.9	1,851.6	2,758.5	32.9
1985	760.7	2,001.3	2,762.0	27.5

Source: The figures for 1972-1974 were obtained from Republic of Trinidad and Tobago, Report of the Committee to Review Government Expenditure (Trinidad and Tobago: The Government Printery, 1978),   p. 37.   The figures for 1975-1985 were obtained from Republic of Trinidad and Tobago, Review of the Economy, 1981. All financial figures have been converted from T.T. dollars to U.S. dollars.

Table 2.7   Government Participation in Commercial Enterprises as a
Percentage of Total Government Revenues, 1973-1983
(millions of U.S. dollars)

YEAR	(1) GOVERNMENT CONTRIBUTION TO INDUSTRY	(2) TOTAL GOVERNMENT REVENUES	(3) GOV'T CONTRIBUTION TO INDUSTRY AS A PERCENTAGE OF TOTAL GOV'T REVENUES
1973	16.2	253.0	6.4
1974	72.4	675.9	10.7
1975	70.1	851.9	8.2
1976	146.0	945.0	15.4
1977	200.4	1,246.0	16.1
1978	230.1	1,302.6	17.7
1979	304.9	1,691.6	18.0
1980	442.3	2,706.6	16.3
1981	554.5	2,914.4	19.0
1982	609.0	2,965.8	20.5
1983	420.9	2,734.8	15.4

Source: The Government of Trinidad and Tobago, Accounting for the Petrodollar 1973-
1983 (Port-of-Spain, Trinidad and Tobago: The Government Printery, 1984), p. 28.
All financial figures have been converted from T.T. dollars to U.S. dollars.

government's officially published figure for people employed by DEWD was
10,500,[10] this figure is highly suspect. In 1982, officials in the salaries section
of the Ministry of Works estimated this figure to be over 50,000. The
program is a very controversial one, particularly because it is widely
perceived as a program utilized to dispense patronage to supporters of the
ruling party. Given the controversial nature of the program, the government
did have an interest in understating the true figure. If the 50,000 figure for
DEWD is used, then the PNM government provided employment to about
one-third of the labor force. Again, the government could carry such a
sizable number of people on its payroll largely because of the revenues
coming in from the petroleum industry.

Further, in order to upgrade the standard of living of the average
Trinidadian citizen, the PNM government spent an enormous amount of
money on a variety of subsidies. These included subsidies on basic food
items, agriculture, utilities, welfare, housing, petroleum products, and
cement. Table 2.8 shows the subsidies provided by the government over the
period 1973 to 1983. The magnitude of these subsidies increased every year,
from US$18.1 million in 1973 to US$634.6 million in 1983, representing an

increase of over 3400 percent. These subsidies will be politically difficult to remove. The point here is that such a high level of subsidization was sustained because of the revenues arising from the petroleum industry.

Table 2.8   Government Subsidies as a Percentage
of Total Revenues, 1973-1983

YEAR	VALUE OF SUBSIDIES (millions of U.S. dollars)	TOTAL GOVERNMENT REVENUES (millions of U.S. dollars)	SUBSIDIES AS A PERCENTAGE OF TOTAL GOVERNMENT REVENUES
1973	18.1	253.0	7.2
1974	62.2	675.9	9.2
1975	69.9	851.9	8.2
1976	98.0	945.0	10.4
1977	133.1	1,246.3	10.7
1978	177.1	1,302.6	13.6
1979	315.0	1,691.6	18.6
1980	415.9	2,706.6	15.4
1981	467.6	2,914.4	16.0
1982	619.1	2,965.8	20.9
1983	634.6	2,734.8	23.2

Source: Government of the Republic of Trinidad and Tobago, Accounting for the Petrodollar 1973-1983 (Port-of-Spain, Trinidad and Tobago: The Government Printery, 1984), p. 72.

Within Trinidad, the signs of prosperity have been everywhere. Construction, both residential and commercial, boomed. Shopping malls mushroomed around the major towns, and fast food establishments flourished. By the mid-1970s, Trinidad had become a truly materialistic society. The drive to acquire modern household goods and appliances took Trinidadians overseas. Weekend shopping sprees to Miami became fashionable, and family vacations to the United States were common. Table 2.9 shows the expenditures on foreign travel by Trinidadians over the period 1973-1983. The amount spent on overseas vacations consistently exceeded 50 percent of the total expenditure on foreign travel annually, and for the period 1979 to 1983, overseas vacation travel averaged approximately 66 percent of the total. As the saying went, money was no problem, and consumption was the order of the day. In fact, Jamaican Prime Minister

Table 2.9 Expenditure on Foreign Travel by Trinidadian Residents,
1973-1983 (millions of U.S. dollars)

YEAR	VACATION	% OF TOTAL	BUSINESS	% OF TOTAL	MEDICAL	% OF TOTAL	EDUCATION	% OF TOTAL	TOTAL
1973	12.8	54.9	3.4	14.6	0.5	2.1	6.6	28.3	23.3
1974	12.4	50.2	4.4	17.8	0.8	3.2	7.1	28.7	24.7
1975	15.2	51.2	6.0	20.2	0.7	2.3	7.8	26.3	29.7
1976	18.8	51.4	6.8	18.6	1.2	3.3	9.8	27.8	36.6
1977	25.7	50.3	10.9	21.3	2.1	4.1	12.4	24.3	51.1
1978	35.0	53.2	13.3	20.2	2.7	4.1	14.7	22.4	65.7
1979	63.6	63.1	14.7	14.6	3.2	3.2	19.3	19.1	100.8
1980	89.2	65.2	17.5	12.8	4.9	3.6	25.3	18.5	130.9
1981	107.7	67.4	18.6	11.6	6.3	3.9	27.3	17.1	159.9
1982	155.1	69.5	19.1	8.6	9.4	4.2	39.5	17.7	223.1
1983	172.1	67.3	21.2	8.3	13.9	5.4	48.4	18.9	255.6

Source: Government of the Republic of Trinidad and Tobago, Accounting For the Petrodollar 1973-1983, (Port-of-Spain, Trinidad and Tobago: The Government Printery, 1984), p. 99.

Michael Manley is reputed to have commented that money was flowing through Trinidad like a dose of Epsom salts!

The preceding sections emphasize the "essentiality" of petroleum to the economy of Trinidad. The petroleum sector has been the main engine of growth of the economy. Petroleum revenues permitted the PNM government to subsidize several industries and to underwrite a number of social programs. There developed in Trinidad what Franklin Tugwell has called, in the case of Venezuela, "an institutionalized addiction to rapidly expanding public resources."[11] The impact of a disruption of the revenues from the oil industry would be enormous. The PNM government naturally recognized this and formulated its petroleum policy with caution. As we will see later in this study, the government successfully attempted to insulate the petroleum sector from domestic political forces.

NOTES

1. Jan Knippers Black et al., Area Handbook for Trinidad and Tobago (Washington, D.C.: The American University, 1976), pp. 1, 33-36. See also Eric E. Williams, History of the People of Trinidad and Tobago (Port-of-Spain, Trinidad: PNM Publishing Co., Ltd., 1962).

2. The World Bank defines middle-income developing countries as those with a per capita income of more than $400 (U.S.). See the World Bank, World Development Report, 1986 (New York: Oxford University Press, 1986), p. 175.

3. Black et al., Area Handbook for Trinidad and Tobago, p. 207.

4. One of the principal features of an open economy is that the long-term rate of growth is largely determined by one exogenous variable (exports). For a further discussion, see Dudley Seers, "The Stages of Economic Growth of a Primary Producer in the Middle of the Twentieth Century," in Robert I. Rhodes, ed., Imperialism and Underdevelopment: A Reader (New York: Monthly Review Press, 1970).

5. Public Relations Division, Whitehall, Facts on Trinidad and Tobago (Port-of-Spain, Trinidad: The Government Printery, 1977), p. 30.

6. Central Statistical Office, Annual Statistical Abstract, 1978 (Port-of-Spain, Trinidad: The Central Statistical Office Printing Unit, 1979), p. 86.

7. Caroni Limited, Directors: Report and Accounts (Port-of-Spain, Trinidad: Caroni Limited, 1977).

8. Republic of Trinidad and Tobago, Annual Statistical Digest 1985, p. 81; and Republic of Trinidad and Tobago, Review of the Economy 1982, p. 76.

9. Republic of Trinidad and Tobago, Annual Statistical Digest 1985, p. 81.

10. Republic of Trinidad and Tobago, Review of the Economy 1979, p. 16.

11. Franklin Tugwell, The Politics of Oil in Venezuela (Stanford: Stanford University Press, 1975), p. 3.

3 ORGANIZATION OF THE PETROLEUM INDUSTRY IN TRINIDAD

Trinidad is one of the oldest oil producers in the world. The first successful oil well in the world was drilled in Trinidad in 1857.[1] Sir Walter Raleigh is known to have taken an interest in Trinidadian pitch. However, attempts at commercial production did not commence until the latter part of the nineteenth century, and successful commercial production did not start until the early 1900s.

The major boost to oil development in the island came in 1910, when the British Admiralty decided to switch from coal to oil as fuel for its ocean-going ships. Large orders were made for Trinidadian oil, and numerous companies became registered for the purpose of tapping the island's oil resources, though only a few of these ever achieved commercial success. Some of the earliest companies involved in oil exploration and production were Trinidad Leaseholds Limited; the United British Oilfields Limited, supported by the Shell Group; Apex Trinidad Oilfields Limited; Kern Trinidad Oilfields; and the Trinidad Petroleum Development Company.[2]

Some significant changes of ownership began to take place in the industry just before the country became independent. In 1956, Trinidad Leaseholds Ltd. was acquired by Texaco Inc. and renamed Texaco Trinidad Inc. In 1956, United British Oilfields Ltd. was renamed Shell Trinidad Ltd. During the same year, British Petroleum came to Trinidad after it acquired the Trinidad Petroleum Development Company. A few years later in 1961, the Pan American Oil Company (later renamed Amoco Trinidad Oil Company), a subsidiary of Standard Oil of Indiana, entered Trinidad and began exploring for oil. In the same year also, British Petroleum had acquired Kern Trinidad Oilfields and Apex Trinidad Oilfields.[3]

Until 1969, all aspects of the oil industry were owned and controlled by foreign companies. Since that time, the government of Trinidad and Tobago has acquired substantial ownership interests in the industry.

Table 3.1 Reserves to Production Ratios, 1962-1985

END OF YEAR	PROVEN OIL RESERVES (1,000 barrels)	PRODUCTION (1,000 barrels)	RESERVES TO PRODUCTION RATIO
1962	425,000	48,876	8.7
1963	425,000	48,678	8.7
1964	425,000	49,731	8.5
1965	425,000	48,859	8.7
1966	425,000	56,603	7.5
1967	525,000	64,995	8.1
1968	525,000	66,904	7.8
1969	590,000	57,418	10.3
1970	605,000	51,048	11.9
1971	*1,053,000	47,147	22.3
1972	560,000	51,212	10.9
1973	500,000	60,670	8.2
1974	651,000	68,136	9.6
1975	651,000	78,621	8.3
1976	650,000	77,672	8.4
1977	650,000	83,620	7.8
1978	650,000	83,778	7.8
1979	655,000	78,258	8.4
1980	650,000	77,618	8.4
1981	561,000	69,119	8.1
1982	633,000	64,617	9.8
1983	600,000	58,344	10.3
1984	538,000	62,042	8.7
1985	610,000	64,259	9.5

Source: Production figures compiled from the Central Statistical Office, Annual Statistical Digest (various issues); proven oil reserves figures from World Oil (various issues).

* This figure was seriously disputed by officials in the Ministry of Energy. Officials claimed that it was closer to 600,000.

However, it is still accurate to say that the petroleum industry in Trinidad continues to be foreign-dominated.

ORGANIZATION OF THE INDUSTRY

Production

Trinidad is a marginal producer of petroleum when compared with overall world production. Production peaked in 1978 at about 83.8 million barrels (see Table 3.1). This was only about 0.4 percent of total world production for that year. And officials in the Ministry of Energy openly acknowledged that the world would not suffer any hardship as a result of a disruption of Trinidadian production.

Not only has Trinidad's annual production been small, but so also have been its proven reserves. Table 3.1 shows the reserves to production ratios for the period 1962 to 1985. These ratios, in effect, give the number of years that production could continue at its present level before the reserves would be completely depleted, and have been characteristically small in the case of Trinidad. They have also generated a sense of insecurity within Trinidad about the duration of the benefits arising from this industry. As a result, Trinidadians are unwilling to undergo the lengthy training required to fill the higher-level technical positions within the industry.

This problem was a source of concern to senior officials at the Ministry of Energy who were interviewed by the author. One official pointed out that the country lacked a broad base in the sciences. It was difficult to cater to the technical needs of the industries located at Point Lisas,[4] as well as to the petroleum industry. It was pointed out that there was no oceanographic institute in Trinidad even though the emphasis in production had shifted to marine fields. It was only in 1975 that a petroleum engineering department was set up at the University of the West Indies at St. Augustine, Trinidad. Shortly afterwards, a petroleum-testing laboratory was also set up. Petroleum-related research and development started in the late 1970s.

Addressing some of the more specific deficiencies, a senior official in the Ministry of Energy said, "There has never been enough [petroleum] engineers. . . . The condition of the industry does not attract petroleum engineers."[5] Petroleum engineers who do come into the industry are fresh out of school and have no experience. A major explanation for the dearth of skilled personnel is found in the Mustofi Commission Report, which was published in 1964. It was a comprehensive examination of the petroleum industry at that time. The report had a tremendous impact not only on the way in which the PNM government approached the industry but also on public attitudes toward the industry.

The Mustofi Report (examined in greater detail in Chapter 6) presented a very bleak picture of the long-term prospects of the Trinidadian oil industry. It did not see Trinidad remaining a producer beyond a decade unless newer oil fields were discovered. Since the publication of the report, the local press, in its regular reporting on the state of the oil industry, has kept the public attuned to the paucity of proven oil reserves.

The feeling existed within the PNM government that Trinidadians could not handle Amoco's marine operations. Not only did the country not have the expertise to operate in the deeper parts of the ocean, it also lacked experience with the type of logistics that are an essential part of offshore production. Neither could the country independently conduct the exploration for oil. Trinidad lacks geophysicists and does not have the facilities in Trinidad to process geophysical data. This is usually done in England by Western Geophysics, an Anglo-American consulting firm.

Officials at the Ministry of Energy also felt that the country needed more refinery inspectors. In the early 1980s, inspection was done by customs officials who did not have extensive training in the chemical aspects of refining. Several officials in Trinidad's Ministry of Energy believed that Texaco might have been exploiting this situation several years ago. Some officials believed that Texaco used to introduce a dye into the lighter and more valuable end products of its refinery and pass these off to Trinidadian customs officials as lesser-valued petroleum products. These were then shipped to the United States, where the dye was removed by a relatively simple process.

The oil industry has also been deprived of highly trained nationals as a result of a "brain drain" from Trinidad. Every year, the Trinidadian government awards scholarships to graduating high school students to enable them to study overseas to become petroleum engineers, petroleum inspectors, or geologists. At the completion of their training, these people are required by contract to return to Trinidad to work for the government for a period of five years. When the contract period is up, many of these technical people typically leave government service to take up employment with the foreign oil companies operating in Trinidad. Salaries at these companies are usually higher than those paid by the government. Thus, the prospect of working for the private oil companies acted as an inducement for people on scholarship overseas to return to Trinidad at the end of their training. However, in the mid-1970s, the PNM government moved to prevent the oil companies from hiring technical personnel serving with the government. The result has been that people on scholarships rarely return home. Most of them find lucrative jobs overseas and repay the government the cost of their scholarships. This, of course, subverts the government's efforts to increase the indigenous pool of technical skills, and the government continues to depend on the technical services offered by the foreign oil companies.

There is one other characteristic of the Trinidadian oil industry that should be noted before we look at the various companies involved in the area of production. From the point of view of oil production, the geological structure in which Trinidad's oil is found is complex. Unlike neighboring Venezuela, the petroleum in Trinidad is not found in large reservoirs. Instead, because of subsurface faulting, the subterranean reservoirs are broken into small, non-continuous reservoirs. Locating these reservoirs becomes a difficult and expensive exercise, since a larger number of wells must be sunk, and production per well is low. Production from existing fields has been declining, and expensive enhanced-recovery methods are being used to coax the remaining petroleum out of existing wells. One result of this is that production costs in Trinidad are relatively high and, until 1973, the oil companies used this fact to squeeze concessions from the Trinidadian government.

Production has shifted over the past decade to offshore areas. The technology employed there is much more sophisticated, and operating conditions are much more difficult. Amoco dominates marine production. However, no new major marine fields have been found since 1972.

There were five major producing companies in Trinidad at the end of 1984. Their annual production figures are shown in Table 3.2. There are some smaller companies such as Trinidad Canadian Oilfield and Premier Consolidated, but their production levels are negligible and are omitted from the general discussion. The five major companies were:

Table 3.2   Production of Crude Petroleum by Company
(millions of barrels), 1967-1983

YEAR	TEXACO	TRINTOC (SHELL until 1974)	TRINIDAD TESORO (BP until 1969)	TNA	AMOCO
1967	29.5	4.2	9.6	20.4	--
1968	29.6	3.6	8.4	24.2	--
1969	20.6	3.3	7.4	25.3	--
1970	16.1	3.0	7.1	24.1	--
1971	13.7	3.2	7.5	22.0	--
1972	--	--	--	--	--
1973	10.0	2.6	8.2	18.9	20.6
1974	8.9	2.4	7.9	19.0	29.5
1975	6.8	2.2	6.5	17.5	45.5
1976	7.7	2.6	6.8	17.5	43.0
1977	7.2	3.0	6.9	16.9	49.4
1978	6.6	3.2	7.4	16.2	50.3
1979	6.8	3.3	7.9	16.1	44.8
1980	6.8	3.1	9.1	14.5	43.9
1981	5.9	2.8	8.8	13.6	37.7
1982	5.5	2.8	8.3	13.9	29.8
1983	4.1	2.0	7.8	13.6	33.9

Source: Figures for 1967-1971 were obtained from T. M. A. Farrell, "The Multinational Corporations, the Petroleum Industry and Economic Underdevelopment in Trinidad and Tobago," doctoral dissertation, Department of Economics, Cornell University, 1974. Figures for 1972-1983 are from Trinidad and Tobago, Review of the Economy (1978, 1982, 1984). Reliable figures for 1972 are not available.

1. Amoco Trinidad Oil Company, which has been the largest producer in the country since 1972, derives its crude oil from wells off the east coast of Trinidad;
2. Texaco Trinidad Inc., which used to be the largest land-producing company, but whose production has declined since 1970;
3. Trinidad Tesoro Oil Company, a joint venture between the Trinidadian government and the Tesoro Petroleum Company of Texas, a relatively small oil company. Trinidad Tesoro was established to acquire the holdings of British Petroleum in 1969;
4. Trinidad and Tobago Oil Company (TRINTOC), a fully-owned company of the government of Trinidad and Tobago. TRINTOC was established in 1974, when the government acquired the holdings of Shell Trinidad Ltd., a subsidiary of the Anglo-Dutch major, Shell International;

Table 3.3   Percentage Distribution of Crude Petroleum Production by Company (major companies only), 1973-1983

YEAR	TEXACO	TRINTOC (SHELL until 1974)	TRINIDAD TESORO (BP until 1969)	TNA	AMOCO
1967	45.4	6.5	15.0	31.4	--
1968	44.3	5.4	12.7	36.2	--
1969	35.9	5.8	13.0	44.1	--
1970	31.5	5.9	13.9	47.2	--
1971	29.1	6.8	15.9	46.7	--
1972	--	--	--	--	--
1973	17.0	4.3	13.5	31.1	33.9
1974	13.4	3.6	11.6	27.9	33.3
1975	8.6	2.8	8.3	22.2	57.9
1976	9.9	3.3	8.7	22.5	55.4
1977	8.6	3.6	8.3	20.2	59.1
1978	7.8	3.8	8.9	19.3	60.0
1979	8.7	4.2	10.0	20.7	56.3
1980	8.8	4.0	11.7	18.7	56.6
1981	8.6	4.0	12.8	19.7	54.6
1982	8.7	4.3	12.8	21.4	52.5
1983	7.0	5.0	13.4	23.2	51.2

Source: Computed from Tables 3.1 and 3.2. See also The Republic of Trinidad and Tobago, Review of the Economy 1982, p. 17, and Review of the Economy 1984, p. 17.

5.   Trinidad Northern Areas (TNA), a consortium in which Texaco, Shell, and British Petroleum had equal shares. Trinidad Tesoro took over the British Petroleum shares in 1969, and TRINTOC acquired the Shell shares in 1974.

Tables 3.2 and 3.3 show that since 1973, Amoco has been the single largest producer of crude oil in Trinidad. Over the period 1973 to 1983, Amoco's production averaged approximately 53 percent of the total annual production. Texaco, with its shares of TNA's production, accounted for an average of about 17 percent of total annual production. Together, these two foreign-owned companies accounted for an annual average of over 70 percent of total production.

What should also be clear, particularly after a perusal of Table 3.3, is that production has been declining. Table 3.4 shows the breakdown of total production in terms of land production and marine production for the period 1967 to 1985. Although total production figures prior to 1967 are available, reliable figures showing the method of production are not available, but it may be assumed that the bulk of the annual production came from land wells, since major marine production did not begin until 1972. In any case, as shown in Table 3.4, the decline in land production has been dramatic. Between 1967 and 1981, land production decreased by 60 percent. Marine production, on the other hand, showed an increasing trend until 1978. Marine production overtook land production in 1972, when Amoco began production off the east coast of Trinidad. Since that time, marine production has accounted for the greater proportion of crude oil produced in Trinidad. Over the period 1974 to 1985, marine production accounted for an average of about 76 percent of total production per year.

The shift from land production to marine production has had implications for the bargaining position of the host country. Theodore Moran (see Chapter 1) has argued that as the host country moves up a learning curve of technological and managerial skills, its bargaining position is strengthened relative to the foreign investor. In Trinidad, those who advocate the nationalization of the oil industry have justified their position partly on the confidence that Trinidad now has the skills to run the refineries and the land operations. They point to the fact that the workforce in the oil industry is made up predominantly of Trinidadians and that TRINTOC, which is government-owned, and Trinidad Tesoro, in which the government has majority ownership, have both operated successfully. However, the shift in emphasis to offshore production has involved a change in technology. Trindadian nationals have little experience in marine operations. Thus it seems that just when the host country has reached a sufficiently high point on the learning curve of one type of technological skills, it must restart the climb on another technological learning curve.

The state-owned company TRINTOC has conducted some offshore exploration, but this has been in shallow waters. In deeper acreages, the government must rely on the foreign companies which have access to the technology and the experience and confidence to use it. The result, of course, is that Trinidad continues its technological dependence on the

Table 3.4   Petroleum Mining--Method of Production, 1962-1985

YEAR	TOTAL PRODUCTION (1,000 barrels)	LAND PRODUCTION (1,000 barrels)	PERCENTAGE OF TOTAL	MARINE PRODUCTION (1,000 barrels)	PERCENTAGE OF TOTAL
1962	48,876	-----	-----	-----	-----
1963	48,678	-----	-----	-----	-----
1964	49,731	-----	-----	-----	-----
1965	48,859	-----	-----	-----	-----
1966	55,603	-----	-----	-----	-----
1967	64,995	39,735	61.1	25,260	38.9
1968	66,904	37,865	56.6	29,039	43.4
1969	57,419	28,992	50.5	28,427	49.5
1970	51,047	25,355	49.7	25,692	50.3
1971	47,147	24,214	51.4	22,933	48.6
1972	51,210	21,930	42.8	29,280	57.2
1973	60,670	20,166	33.2	40,504	66.8
1974	68,136	18,790	27.6	49,346	72.4
1975	78,621	15,096	19.2	65,525	72.3
1976	77,672	16,351	21.2	61,321	78.9
1977	83,620	16,414	19.6	67,206	80.4
1978	83,778	16,572	19.8	67,206	80.2
1979	78,258	17,162	21.9	61,096	78.1
1980	77,618	17,108	22.0	60,510	78.0
1981	69,119	16,803	24.3	52,316	75.7
1982	64,617	15,104	23.4	49,513	76.6
1983	58,344	13,777	23.6	44,567	76.4
1984	62,042	13,721	22.2	48,321	77.8
1985	64,259	14,436	22.5	49,823	77.5

Source: The Central Statistical Office, <u>Annual Statistical Digest</u> (several issues).

foreign companies, and nationalization of the marine fields does not make sense given the lack of technical competence to operate them.

Refining

Trinidad has had the capacity of becoming a major refining center. Since independence in 1962, the two major refineries have been modernized and their respective capacities expanded. The TRINTOC refinery at Point Fortin originally had a rated capacity of 100,000 barrels per day. It was geared for crude oil with high sulphur content and low American Petroleum Institute (API) gravity. The PNM government had planned to upgrade this refinery so that it could produce lighter end products. The Point Fortin refinery handles the crude production from the TRINTOC land wells and from Trinidad Tesoro's land operations. However, since the late 1970s, the refinery has been operating below 65 percent of capacity, largely because of TRINTOC's inability to get feedstocks from outside of the country.

The other major refinery is located at Pointe-à-Pierre and was operated by Texaco Trinidad until 1985. It had a rated capacity of 350,000 barrels per day, although by 1982, this had been downgraded to about 240,000 barrels per day. Crude oil from Texaco's land operations was also refined here.

The total refinery capacity available in Trinidad in the late 1970s was 450,000 barrels per day. To keep the refineries operating at full capacity, Trinidad needed about 164.3 million barrels of crude oil annually. However, Trinidad's highest level of production occurred in 1978 and totaled 83.8 million barrels, or only about one-half of what the refineries required to operate at full capacity. Trinidad, therefore, needed to import crude oil from outside. What worsens the refinery situation is that Amoco exports its crude oil directly to the United States, that is, without utilizing the refining facilities in Trinidad. It should be noted here that OPEC classifies Trinidad as a net importer of crude oil and has denied Trinidad membership in the organization on that basis.

As Table 3.5 shows, the refineries in Trinidad have rarely operated close to full capacity, partly reflecting the difficulty of getting crude oil feedstocks. The table also shows that the greater proportion of refinery throughput is accounted for by imports from other sources of crude oil. The imported crude oil is, of course, refined for a fee and then re-exported. Over the period 1967 to 1982, imports accounted for approximately 66 percent of refinery throughput annually. The bulk of these were brought in by Texaco from its subsidiaries in other parts of the world. The refined products were marketed through Texaco's outlets in the United States. Texaco's ability to import crude oil and to market the refined products made the government of Trinidad much more dependent on Texaco than Texaco was on it.

A further look at Table 3.5 reveals that since 1970, the total refinery throughput has been falling. By 1978, almost 50 percent of the total refinery capacity remained idle. There were several reasons for this trend. First, domestic production of crude oil has been declining, necessitating greater volumes of imports annually for the refineries. Second, much of the windfall revenues collected by oil-producing countries as a result of the OPEC price hike after 1973 was invested in refineries, thereby creating an excess of refinery capacity worldwide. Finally, lower prices for refined products were also a contributing factor.

The condition of the refining component of the industry in the late 1970s inspired a lively debate within the PNM government about the advisability of eventual national ownership of the Texaco refinery. Quite apart from the purchase price of the refinery, which was expected to be very high, the future of the refining and marketing operations was worrisome. Most of the oil that passed through the Pointe-à-Pierre refinery was brought into Trinidad from Texaco subsidiaries around the world. Officials in the government recognized that it would be extremely difficult for the government to import crude oil for this refinery, especially since there existed an excess of refinery capacity world-wide.[6] In fact, the government was unable to secure feedstocks for its own refinery at Point Fortin to take advantage of its full operating capacity. Further, since the products of the Texaco refinery were marketed in the United States by Texaco outlets, nationalization of the refinery would not bring with it the benefits of this market. Despite these misgivings, the PNM government was eventually pressured into purchasing the Texaco refinery in 1985 (see Chapter 6).

Table 3.5 Refinery Throughput (barrels), 1967-1984

		THROUGHPUT				REFINERY OUTPUT
YEAR	LOCALLY PRODUCED CRUDE	PERCENTAGE OF TOTAL	IMPORTED CRUDE	PERCENTAGE OF TOTAL	TOTAL	
1967	58,488,004	42.1	80,436,632	57.9	138,924,636	134,707,727
1968	59,835,383	39.6	91,446,715	60.4	151,282,088	146,859,856
1969	50,315,067	32.7	103,761,531	67.3	154,076,598	148,659,189
1970	41,595,465	26.9	113,264,796	73.1	154,860,261	150,258,601
1971	38,679,401	26.6	106,868,559	73.4	145,547,960	141,503,418
1972	37,123,742	25.7	107,149,773	74.3	144,273,516	138,895,094
1973	38,063,033	26.9	103,623,751	73.1	141,686,784	135,812,215
1974	35,347,762	27.0	95,471,942	73.0	130,819,584	127,107,931
1975	30,721,406	35.9	54,938,912	64.1	85,660,318	81,874,278
1976	32,910,827	28.0	84,684,155	72.0	117,594,982	114,304,477
1977	30,825,235	31.2	68,911,245	69.7	98,816,779	8,552,498
1978	28,964,655	33.7	56,917,187	66.3	85,881,842	3,563,081
1979	30,653,530	37.0	52,210,925	63.0	82,864,455	78,484,749
1980	32,139,072	38.0	52,484,475	62.0	84,623,547	82,578,450
1981	24,734,088	39.0	38,609,628	61.0	63,343,717	60,579,297
1982	31,717,207	57.6	23,388,615	42.4	55,105,822	55,481,537
1983	27,178,312	100.0	----------	--	27,178,312	28,536,497
1984	27,433,823	97.5	709,381	2.5	28,143,204	26,435,038

Source: Central Statistical Office, <u>Annual Statistical Digest 1971</u>, <u>Annual Statistical Digest 1978</u>, and <u>Annual Statistical Digest 1985</u>.

Marketing

In the area of marketing, the foreign companies hold a commanding position. As Table 2.5 showed, the greater proportion of exports from the oil sector consists of refined products. The refineries in Trinidad, like several others in the Caribbean, had been established as U.S. offshore refineries. As a result, the product mixes have been geared to meet the requirements of the owners of the refineries and the markets they serviced. Table 3.6 lists the principal products of the Trinidadian refineries. Emphasis has been placed on producing the heavier end products, such as residual fuel oil, which are cheaper. In fact, fuel oil accounts for nearly 60 percent of the total

Table 3.6 Analysis of Refinery Output, 1967-1984

YEAR	TOTAL REFINERY OUTPUT (millions of barrels)	PRINCIPAL PRODUCTS (millions of barrels)									
		Fuel Oil	% of Total	Motor Gaso-line	% of Total	Aviation Turbine Fuel	% of Total	Gas/ Diesel Oil	% of Total	Kerosene	% of Total
1967	134.7	75.0	55.7	19.6	14.6	11.7	8.7	19.5	14.4	3.7	2.7
1968	146.9	84.9	57.8	20.9	14.2	15.3	10.4	18.4	12.5	3.7	2.5
1969	148.7	88.3	59.4	21.7	14.6	15.1	10.2	16.6	11.2	2.5	1.7
1970	150.3	91.4	60.8	20.8	13.9	12.4	8.3	15.5	10.3	6.4	4.3
1971	141.5	79.3	56.0	22.9	16.2	11.5	8.1	18.7	13.2	5.8	4.0
1972	138.9	85.4	61.5	20.1	14.5	19.5	6.8	13.8	9.9	6.8	4.9
1973	135.8	81.9	60.3	19.6	14.4	8.4	6.2	15.3	12.3	7.8	5.7
1974	127.1	74.5	58.6	18.7	14.7	8.4	6.6	14.9	11.7	6.1	4.8
1975	81.9	47.5	58.1	14.0	17.0	4.0	4.8	10.8	13.1	3.9	4.7
1976	114.3	66.8	58.4	20.0	17.5	4.3	3.7	12.2	10.6	6.8	6.0
1977	98.6	56.4	57.2	19.0	19.3	2.5	2.5	10.7	10.9	5.8	5.9
1978	83.6	45.5	54.4	16.8	20.1	2.2	2.7	10.1	12.1	4.5	5.4
1979	79.6	43.5	54.6	14.8	18.6	2.3	2.9	11.7	14.7	3.2	4.0
1980	82.5	42.7	51.8	15.1	18.3	3.2	3.9	13.8	16.7	3.2	3.9
1981	60.6	29.6	48.8	13.0	21.5	1.3	2.1	10.3	17.0	2.1	3.5
1982	55.5	27.4	49.4	11.2	20.2	2.5	4.5	9.5	17.1	1.5	2.7
1983	28.5	14.5	50.9	8.4	29.5	2.0	7.0	4.5	15.8	1.1	3.9
1984	26.4	14.6	55.3	6.0	22.7	1.9	7.2	4.2	15.9	1.2	4.5

Source: Central Bank of Trinidad and Tobago, <u>Monthly Statistical Digest</u> 14 (September 1981), p. 57; Central Statistical Office, <u>Annual Statistical Digest 1985</u>, p. 125.

annual output of the refineries. The market for this product is the northeastern United States, where it is used for heating purposes during the winter. There was great domestic clamor for increasing the proportion of lighter end products coming out of the Texaco refinery since they would fetch higher prices, but the output from the Texaco refinery continued to respond solely to the requirements of the U.S. market. In fact, Texaco's installation of a desulphurization plant (rated capacity of 100,000 barrels per day) at its Pointe-à-Pierre refinery was a response to anti-pollution legislation in the United States. Thus Texaco's policies in Trinidad responded to market conditions for petroleum and petroleum products in the United States, even though these policies were not in the best interests of Trinidad.

Further, the marketing experience of the state-owned company TRINTOC created doubts in the minds of government officials about the country's ability to market its petroleum and petroleum products in the event that the entire industry came under state-ownership. TRINTOC handles the marketing of the refined products from its refinery at Point Fortin. Crude oil for this refinery is supplied by the TRINTOC oil wells, but TRINTOC also buys all the crude oil produced by Trinidad Tesoro from its land operations. In its marketing operations, Trinidad assumes the role of an independent. It markets petroleum products to the Eastern Caribbean, South America (the Guianas, in particular), and the United States. TRINTOC sustained severe losses in its U.S. marketing operations in 1981. This was largely due to the fact that the price of its principal product, fuel oil, was hovering at about $25 a barrel, whereas the price of TRINTOC's crude oil was about $31. TRINTOC was also required to pay U.S. tariffs on its fuel oil. Also, TRINTOC has only been able to secure short-term contracts in the United States. This has raised fears that if Trinidad acquired control over its oil industry, it could find itself as a supplier of last resort. Thus the experience of TRINTOC, particularly with regard to marketing outside of the Caribbean, dampened any enthusiasm PNM government officials might have had about acquiring complete ownership of the industry, or of any other company within the industry.

TRINTOC's experience also accounted for the attitude of some officials who lauded the country's association with oil companies that were integrated from the well-head to the gas pumps. Amoco has benefited from this type of attitude in governmental circles. Amoco, which is the single largest producer of crude oil in Trinidad, exports all of its crude oil to the United States. Amoco's crude oil, obtained from marine fields, is of very high quality with a low sulphur content and high API gravity. Amoco also buys the marine-produced crude oil from Trinidad Tesoro and exports it to the United States. The crude oil is refined in the United States and sold through Amoco's outlets. Amoco's justification for its action, which was accepted by the PNM government and has not been questioned by the NAR government, is that it is providing the government with a secure market in the United States.

The Trinidadian domestic market for petroleum products, which was formerly controlled by foreign companies, became a government monopoly in 1976. The state-owned National Petroleum Marketing Company (NPMC) handles local demand for petroleum products, primarily gasoline. The government owns all of the local gas stations and operates them through the NPMC. In 1969, when the PNM government bought out British Petroleum, it acquired the British Petroleum gas stations. Similarly, in 1974, the PNM government acquired control over all of the Shell gas stations. With these gas stations under its control, the government approached Texaco with a proposal to purchase the remaining gas stations owned by Texaco. Texaco refused to sell. However, the government was selling gas at its stations at subsidized prices. This resulted in a virtual boycott of the higher-priced gas available at the Texaco gas stations. Finally, in 1976, Texaco consented to sell its gas stations to the government.

Exploration

Exploration is the costliest aspect of the petroleum business. It is also the area that carries the greatest risk. As Edith Penrose points out, in the case of a capital-poor, developing country, exploration for oil is best left to the larger international companies.[7] The financial and technological resources at the disposal of these companies make their chances of discovering the country's oil reserves much greater than if the country undertook the task alone. Both the PNM government and its successor accepted this reasoning. As Kelvin Ramnath, former Minister of Energy in the NAR government, put it, "Exploration on the east coast is a very expensive type of operation. You've got to have a lot of money to continue your exploration program."[8] Referring to the technological aspect of exploration, he said:

We don't have the capability, as a state, through a nationalized company, say a local Trinidad and Tobago oil company, to do that kind of work. It requires extensive seismic lines and interpretation, and the drilling of wells in an environment that has no history of oil production.[9]

Except for a limited exploration effort by the state-owned company TRINTOC, the bulk of the oil exploration is carried out by foreign companies. The major foreign companies involved in exploration operations are: Agip, incorporated in Italy; Deminex, incorporated in Germany; and Amoco, Tenneco, Occidental Petroleum Corporation, and Mobil Oil Corporation, all of which are incorporated in the United States.

Despite intense exploration activity, no major commercial oil discovery has been made. The last major oil discovery was made off the east coast of Trinidad in 1969 by Amoco, which has been producing from those fields since 1972. However, large reservoirs of natural gas have been discovered. Tenneco, in combination with Texaco, found gas off the east coast of Trinidad, and DATO, a joint venture of Deminex, Agip, Tenneco, and Occidental, found gas off the north coast. These gas finds and the huge gas reserves that had previously been discovered by Amoco convinced the PNM government that its future lay in natural gas production. Nevertheless, the high oil prices of the 1970s and the hope that these prices might rise again in the 1980s serve as an incentive for continued exploration.

It was clear to the PNM government that exploration was absolutely essential for future production. Since the country did not have the technological capability to independently conduct the exploration, and since the government was unwilling to commit the extensive financial resources to the exploration effort, it tried to attract foreign companies to engage in exploration. Concerns about exploration served as a deterrent to nationalization of foreign producing companies. As a former Minister of Energy explained, "You could not take the posture that you were interested in nationalizing and then look for multinationals to come in and explore."[10]

INDUSTRY CONSTRAINTS ON NATIONAL OWNERSHIP

In this chapter, we have examined the organization of the petroleum industry in Trinidad through 1984. Although the Trinidadian government had a significant presence in the oil industry by virtue of its ownership of TRINTOC and its majority holdings in Trinidad Tesoro, the industry continued to be dominated by foreign companies. The case was made that Trinidad was much more dependent on these companies than they were on Trinidad.

The main producer of crude oil in Trinidad is Amoco Trinidad, a subsidiary of Standard Oil of Indiana. The emergence of Amoco as the main producer paralleled the shift from land production to offshore production. Offshore production requires technology that has not yet been "learned" in Trinidad. Thus there continues to be a "technological gap" in the Trinidadian oil industry, and the host country continues its technology dependence on the foreign companies.

Until 1982, Trinidad was much more important as a refining center than as a producer of crude petroleum. In the refining sphere of the industry in Trinidad, Texaco occupied the dominant position. It controlled more than 75 percent of the country's total refining capacity, but more importantly, it was able to secure feedstocks for its Trinidadian refinery from subsidiaries in other parts of the world and was able to market the refined products through its outlets in the United States. This made the government of Trinidad much more dependent on Texaco than Texaco was on it.

In the area of marketing, the performance of the state-owned oil company TRINTOC has not been very impressive, at least outside of the Caribbean. This alerted the government of Trinidad to the magnitude of the marketing difficulties it would encounter if it nationalized the entire industry. The experience of the state-owned company seemed to counsel a retention of the status quo in the Trinidadian oil industry.

Trinidad continues to rely on foreign companies to conduct exploration for new oil fields because it can ill afford the enormous capital outlay such activity requires, and it does not have the technical capability to do the exploration. However, since 1969, there has been no major commercial oil discovery in Trinidad. This fact, coupled with the marginality of Trinidadian oil production (compared with that of the rest of the world) was a source of alarm to government officials concerned with the oil industry. It increased their reluctance to control, by way of nationalization, plants and equipment that would be very costly to acquire and that would become obsolete in a relatively short time when the oil ran out.

In the previous chapter, we discussed the essentiality of the petroleum industry to the Trinidadian economy. Not only has the petroleum industry been the principal engine of growth in the economy, but oil revenues, particularly after 1973, have allowed the government to engage in a massive subsidization program in industry and social welfare. Given the country's dependence on petroleum revenues, it appeared self-evident that governmental policy affecting the oil industry would be formulated with caution.

While the revenues from oil were enormous and while the economy grew enormously after 1973, Trinidad remained a minor oil producer with very little impact on the international oil industry. It continued to depend on foreign companies for technology, both in production and continuing exploration. It continued to depend on foreign companies for crude oil to keep its refineries in operation, and most importantly, for markets for its petroleum and petroleum products. The absence of any new major oil fields portends a bleak future for the Trinidadian oil industry. These considerations alone would suggest that nationalization of the oil industry was never a realistic option for the PNM government.

However, as Smith and Wells point out, governments may be forced by domestic political pressures to make demands on foreign companies that neither their bargaining strength nor their economic interests warrant.[11] In the next two chapters, we will look at the types of domestic pressures that were brought on the PNM government to alter its policies toward foreign investment in general, and the oil industry in particular.

NOTES

1. Jan Knippers Black et al., Area Handbook for Trinidad and Tobago (Washington, D.C., 1976), p. 221.

2. Ministry of Energy, History of Oil in Trinidad, Appendix I, (undated), p. 1.

3. Trevor M.A. Farrell, "The Multinational Corporations, the Petroleum Industry and Economic Underdevelopment in Trinidad and Tobago," Ph.D. dissertation, Cornell University, 1974, pp. 99-100.

4. Point Lisas is the site of most of the newer industries.

5. Interview, Ministry of Energy, Port-of-Spain, Trinidad, February 16, 1982.

6. Ibid. For an official government view of the trend the Trinidadian oil industry is likely to take in the near future, see Trevor M. Boopsingh, "The Petroleum Industry--the Next Decade," Ministry of Energy and Energy-Based Industries, Trinidad and Tobago, January 1, 1980; and the Conference Report on Best Uses of Our Petroleum Resources, Vol. 1 (undated). The conference was held at Chaguaramas from January 13 to January 15, 1975 and was sponsored by the government of Trinidad and Tobago.

7. Edith Penrose, The Large International Firm in Developing Countries: The International Petroleum Industry (Cambridge, Mass.: The M.I.T. Press, 1968), pp. 236-238.

8. Interview with Kelvin Ramnath, former Minister of Energy (January 1987-March 1988) on May 7, 1988 in New York City.

9. Ibid.

10. Ibid.

11. David A. Smith and Louis T. Wells, Jr., <u>Negotiating Third World Mineral Agreements, Promise as Prologue</u> (Cambridge, Mass.: Ballinger, 1975), p. 18.

4 THE ETHNIC BASIS OF POLITICS IN TRINIDAD

A hypothesis that enjoys widespread acceptance among scholars studying the relations between the multinational corporation and the developing host country is that as the foreign-controlled industry increases in importance to the economy, the foreign investors in that industry become objects of attack by nationalistic groups within the country. The increasing visibility of the foreign companies causes domestic political and economic groups to closely monitor and criticize their behavior. This is especially true if the foreign-controlled industry is a mineral-extracting industry and if it dominates the economy of the host country.

In Trinidad, economic nationalism has always been strong within the oil union and has been intermittently injected into the political system by the union or by parties affiliated with the union. However, until 1970, the efforts of the oil union notwithstanding, the foreign companies in both oil and sugar enjoyed tremendous insulation from the domestic politics of the country.

Several factors accounted for this situation. First, the major land-producing oil companies, Texaco, Shell, and British Petroleum, as well as the sugar company, Caroni Ltd., entered Trinidad when it was under a colonial regime. Trinidad did not acquire its political independence from Britain until 1962. Second, although indigenous leaders began to play an increasing role in the governing of the colony following World War II, the executive was selected by the British governor and was generally pro-business in its orientation. Even the People's National Movement (PNM), which achieved political office in 1956 and enjoyed greater autonomy in the running of the colony, favored foreign enterprise.

However, one of the major reasons for the "splendid isolation" of the foreign companies was the peculiar nature of domestic politics in Trinidad. The prospect of independence from Britain stimulated intense maneuvering among indigenous leaders for control of the machinery of government. In this struggle, race emerged as the principal determinant of party loyalty. The PNM secured political office in 1956 by portraying itself as the champion of the black and mixed black segments of the population. The People's Democratic Party (PDP) championed the cause of the Indians in Trinidad. The race question so dominated the domestic political agenda that the foreign companies were generally ignored. Nevertheless, race guaranteed the PNM security of tenure. The PNM won every national election between 1956 and 1986.[1] Under PNM control, the state functioned for about a decade as tax collector, and the party used the enormous patronage potential of the state to reward its followers and thereby ensure their allegiance.

This chapter looks at the struggle for control of the post-colonial state and the role that ethnicity played in this struggle. Ironically, as Chapter 5 will show, it was the race variable that eventually forced national attention to the dominant role of foreign enterprise in the Trinidadian economy.

EARLY POLITICAL MOBILIZATION

As Table 4.1 shows, Trinidad is an ethnically heterogeneous society, a legacy of colonialism and a plantation system of agricultural organization. The vast majority of the population are descendants of transplanted peoples. The two principal mechanisms of immigration into the colony were slavery and the indenture system. These explain the presence of the two largest ethnic groups, the Africans and the East Indians, in the country. It is between these two groups that ethnic rivalry has been most intense.

In large measure, the settlement pattern of Trinidad was historically similar to that of the other Caribbean islands. Under Spanish rule, Trinidad was virtually ignored since Spain was far more interested in the mineral-rich areas of the New World. The enslavement of the indigenous Indians on the island led to a rapid decline in their numbers, and, in the eighteenth century, Africans were brought to the island as slaves to boost the production of tobacco and coffee. However, it was not until the last quarter of the century that settlement and agricultural productivity showed dramatic increases due to a change in Spanish colonial policy which opened up the island to immigration. French planters and their slaves came in large numbers from other Caribbean islands and began sugar cane cultivation. When the British finally secured control of Trinidad in 1803, the French constituted the largest European group on the island, but the Africans were a numerical majority.

With the emancipation of the slaves in 1834, a shortage of labor for the sugar plantations developed. The problem was resolved by the introduction of indentured labor from Hong Kong, Portuguese Madeira, and India. The majority of the indentured laborers came from India. In fact, when the indenture system was brought to an end in 1917, the Indians in Trinidad accounted for about one-third of the total population.

Indentured Indians became the bulk of the labor force on the sugar plantations. The majority of the unindentured Indians took up some form of agriculture. This pattern of agricultural employment continued after the system of indenture was brought to an end in 1917, though Indians began to move into commerce and the legal and medical professions.

Blacks moved out of the sugar plantations in two general directions. Many moved into and around Port-of-Spain, where they found employment as craftworkers and wage laborers. With increasing education, blacks began to enter the civil service, the police force, and the teaching, legal, and medical professions. The other pattern of migration was due south into the burgeoning oil industry, where blacks became the backbone of this industry.

Table 4.1 Ethnic Composition of the Population of Trinidad and Tobago

ETHNIC GROUP	1946	% OF TOTAL	1960	% OF TOTAL	1970	% OF TOTAL	1980	% OF TOTAL
BLACK	261,485	46.9	358,588	43.3	398,765	42.8	430,864	40.8
EAST INDIAN	195,747	35.1	301,946	36.5	373,538	40.1	429,187	40.7
WHITE	15,283	2.7	15,718	1.9	11,383	1.2	9,946	0.9
CHINESE	5,641	1.0	8,361	1	7,962	0.8	5,562	0.5
MIXED	78,775	14.1	134,749	16.3	131,904	14.2	172,285	16.3
SYRIAN/ LEBANESE/ OTHERS	889	0.2	8,595	1	7,519	0.8	7,919	0.8
TOTAL	557,970	100	827,957	100	931,071	99.9	1,055,763	100

Source: Central Statistical Office, Annual Statistical Digest 1956, Annual Statistical Digest 1967, Annual Statistical Digest 1978, and Annual Statistical Digest 1985.

The two races, the Africans and the Indians, developed apart from one another. Not only were they separated by occupation with blacks concentrated in the oil industry and government service and Indians in agriculture, but they were also separated physically. Blacks were based in the towns and Indians largely in the rural areas. Culturally, the two races were also different. The Indians resisted assimilation into the new culture. They continued to identify with Indian culture, and they clung to their original religions, Hinduism and Islam, though a small group converted to Christianity. Blacks, on the other hand, practiced Christianity and made an effort to assimilate western culture.

Contact between these two races began to increase as Indians moved into the towns and began to compete with blacks economically. Increasing black militancy against white rule worried the Indians about their future under black rule. At the same time, the rapid rate of increase among the

Indians worried blacks that the Indians might eventually achieve numerical superiority and, with it, political control over blacks. In fact, the comparatively rapid increase in the Indian segment of the population continues to worry blacks today. As Table 4.1 shows, while Indians constituted 35.1 percent of the population in 1946, in 1980, this proportion had increased to 40.7 percent, and the number of Indians in Trinidad in 1980 more than doubled the 1946 number. Blacks, on the other hand, accounted for 46.9 percent of the population in 1946, but only 40.8 percent in 1980. Over the same period, the number of blacks had increased by only 65 percent of the 1946 number.

Nevertheless, the colonial political and social structure kept both ethnic groups in check. The colonial social structure was dominated by Europeans, primarily the French and British. They controlled the political and economic life of the colony. They were followed by the mulattoes who identified strongly with the European culture and spared no effort to move up in the system. At the very bottom were the blacks, East Indians, and Chinese.

Political consciousness developed much earlier among blacks than among East Indians. Blacks accepted Trinidad as their home and made an effort to become integrated into the mainstream of colonial life. However, black aspirations ran up against white domination, which blacks increasingly resented. East Indians on the sugar plantations and in other forms of agriculture were relatively isolated within Trinidad and did not identify as much with Trinidad as they did with India.

Political consciousness among blacks became heightened after World War I. Blacks, who had left Trinidad to serve with the British West Indies Regiment in Europe, had been told that theirs was a crusade to make the world safe for democracy. The European experience shattered many of the myths that had served to buttress British colonial rule, and the Afro-Trinidadians returned home determined to get a better deal from the system. Many returning servicemen became associated with Captain Andrew Cipriani, the white officer who commanded their regiment and who had now entered active politics as a champion of the underdog. He founded the Trinidad Labor Party in 1934. Although he drew the majority of his support from urban blacks, he had succeeded in forging a coalition between blacks and Indians. In fact, a number of prominent Indians, the most notable of whom was Adrian Cola Rienzi, were closely identified with Cipriani. Rienzi, a lawyer with socialist leanings, was in charge of organizing trade union activity in southern Trinidad.[2]

By 1935, there were signs that the Cipriani movement was fragmenting. Cipriani was about 68 years old. He seemed unable to control the mass following he had created and was unwilling to share leadership or to listen to the younger voices in his party. Also, black workers in the oil belt were growing impatient with Cipriani's gradualist policies. Eventually two of his lieutenants, Adrian Cola Rienzi and Tubal Uriah Butler, a black political agitator, broke away from the Trinidad Labor Party and took a sizable proportion of the membership with them.[3]

In 1937, Butler called a general strike in the oil belt. The strike and the accompanying violence resulted in the loss of 14 lives and in the injury of about 59 others. The purpose of the strike was to redress some long-standing grievances of black workers in the oil belt. However, the strike also dramatized the need for social, political, and economic reforms in the colony.[4]

Two important consequences grew out of the 1937 disturbances. The first was the recognition by the colonial authorities of the right of the Trinidadian workers to unionize. Under Adrian Cola Rienzi, who had been the workers' principal negotiator during the strike, two of the most powerful unions in the country's history were established: the Oilfields Workers' Trade Union (OWTU) and the All-Trinidad Sugar Estates and Factory Workers' Trade Union (ATSEFWTU). The OWTU was recognized in 1938, but the ATSEFWTU was not recognized until 1945. Rienzi was the president of both unions, and a great amount of cooperation existed between the unions. Like Cipriani, Rienzi had succeeded in "mixing oil with sugar," that is, forging a coalition between the black oil workers and the Indian sugar workers. The second result of the 1937 strike was that it drew British attention to the need to change the constitutional instruments governing the colony, and this led to the granting of adult suffrage to the colony.[5]

The first election under adult suffrage was held in 1946. The constitution in force at the time allowed nine elected seats in a legislature of 18 members. The other nine members were nominated by the British governor, who exercised veto power over the proceedings of the legislature. Among the numerous political groups and independents that contested the election was the Trades Union Congress, representing a group of labor unions.[6] This is noteworthy because it marked the beginning of a tradition of direct labor involvement in the politics of Trinidad.

Bitter controversy developed over the constitutional arrangements governing the colony, and this led to constitutional reforms that were instituted in 1950. Under the constitution of 1950, the legislature was to be composed of 18 elected members, four ex-officio members, and five nominated members, presided over by an appointed speaker. For the first time, the elected members in the legislature would outnumber the non-elected. The constitution also provided that the Executive Council should become the principal instrument of policy with a ministerial system in which the elected members of the Executive Council would be responsible for the administration of government departments. However, members of the Executive Council were still to be selected by the governor.[7]

The 1950 election was fiercely contested. One hundred and forty-one candidates contested for the 18 available seats. Ninety of these candidates were independents and the other 51 carried a party label of some sort. Six of the independent candidates were successful in winning a seat each. The Caribbean Socialist Party, the Trinidad Labor Party, and the Political Progress Group each won two seats, while the Butler Party, which was an alliance of blacks and Indians, won six seats, the largest number won by any party in the legislature. However, when the members of the Executive Council were selected by the governor, none of the Butlerites was chosen. The feeling was that Butler did not have the administrative and intellectual preparation to execute ministerial duties.[8]

Some common features characterized the elections of 1946 and 1950. Political parties did not demonstrate any permanence. They mushroomed at election time and faded soon afterwards. The parties tended to be a collection of individuals around some central personality. They had little organizational structure and no comprehensive program. In large measure, this was due to constitutional constraints. There was no provision for handing over executive decision-making to the majority party, and this discouraged party cohesion. Finally, although considerable uneasiness surfaced among blacks and Indians, the elections showed that political coalitions between the two ethnic groups were possible. In any event, race as a political variable was not as entrenched as it would become in the late 1950s.

THE EMERGENCE OF A TWO-PARTY SYSTEM

The election of 1956 was a dramatic shift from the two previous ones. The constitution introduced in 1956 promised full internal self-government and gave impetus to the establishment of mass-based parties in Trinidad. The new constitution increased the number of elected members of the legislature to 24. It also provided for the election of a chief minister by the Legislative Council. The chief minister would be the leader of both the Executive Council and the Legislative Council. The Executive Council would consist of ten members, including the chief minister. The number of nominated members of the Executive Council was reduced to two, the colonial secretary and the attorney general, who were ex-officio members. The governor would allocate the ministerial portfolios, but only after consultation with the chief minister. The framers of the 1956 constitution attempted to create a British type of cabinet government.[9] The conditions were now set for political parties to compete for control of the Executive Council.

The People's National Movement (PNM), which was victorious in the 1956 national election, began as the Political Education Group. It was a group of predominantly black professionals who met regularly to discuss the political problems facing Trinidad. The chief spokesman for the group was Dr. Eric Eustace Williams. Williams acquired a reputation in Trinidad as an educator. He had obtained a doctoral degree in history from Oxford University and had taught political science at Howard University in Washington, D.C. In 1948, he took up a research position with the Anglo-American Caribbean Economic Commission, which permitted him to return to the Caribbean. He gave numerous public lectures in Trinidad, many of which dealt with non-political subjects. As a result of these, he became very well known in Trinidad and began to develop a following. He became actively involved in politics in 1955 when his application was turned down for the vacant position of secretary-general of the Caribbean Economic Commission.[10] Williams used this issue to launch his political career. As Selwyn Ryan put it, "His main strategy was to get the masses to regard his personal struggle as their struggle--the struggle of the qualified black West Indian for recognition and advancement."[11] In portraying himself as the restorer of black self-respect, Williams struck a harmonious chord in the minds of the blacks. The issue of black self-respect had been central to the struggle of Butler and his followers in the oil belt. Williams appeared to be a new prophet who would take black consciousness to a higher level.

At Woolford Square in Port-of-Spain, Williams lectured on the origins and consequences of slavery and on the nature of the slave regime and economy. His lectures had a mesmerizing effect on blacks. As Oxaal observes, "For many lower-class Negroes, particularly Creole [black] women, Dr. Williams was nothing less than a messiah come to lead the black children into the Promised Land."[12] However, Oxaal points out that the image of Williams as a racial messiah, though strongest among the black lower class, was by no means also confined to this class. It could also be found in the black middle class.[13]

The People's National Movement was inaugurated on January 15, 1956. It was well organized and presented a comprehensive political program embodied in a party pamphlet called The People's Charter. The Charter called for constitutional reform and outlined a program for the achievement of a welfare state. However, the PNM became regarded as an instrument for the advancement of black interests. As Ryan put it: "Politically conservative Hindus, White settlers and businessmen, the Catholic Church, the old-line trade unions, and political leaders all feared its influence over the black masses."[14] The PNM became the target of attacks from the opposition parties as well as from the independent candidates. The principal charge was that Williams was driving a racial wedge into the community.[15]

The major threat to PNM electoral success in 1956 came from the People's Democratic Party (PDP), a conservative party founded in 1953 by Bhadase Sagan Maraj, an Indian and one of the wealthiest men on the island. Maraj has become a legendary figure in Trinidadian politics. He was not a man with much formal education, but he was tough and pragmatic. Maraj derived his political strength from his control over the Sanatan Dharma Maha Sabha, the umbrella organization of the Hindus, and from his control over the sugar union. His style of politics was essentially clientelist. He built schools and temples in the Indian areas and gave liberally to the poor and needy. As Maraj's political influence among the Indians grew, he was joined by Ashford Sinanan and Mitra Sinanan, two top lawyers in Trinidad, who had already proved themselves as able parliamentarians, and by other politically ambitious Indians. Thus, the Indian-dominated PDP prepared to confront the black-dominated PNM.[16]

There were four other major parties that contested the 1956 election. The Party of Political Progress Groups (POPPG) represented the local white upper and middle classes and was identified with the Chamber of Commerce, the Catholic Church, and the old colonial order. The party accused Williams of subtly invoking black hostilities against whites by periodic resurrections of "slave history." The Trinidad Labor Party (TLP) claimed that, as the party of Cipriani, it was the true heir to the leadership of the working class. The Butler Party argued that Butler was the only leader who had been successful in bridging the gap between the Indians and the blacks. The fourth party was the Caribbean National Labor Party (CNLP) the leadership of which was drawn predominantly from labor unions. The party leader was John Rojas, who was also the president of the Oilfields Workers' Trade Union. The party advocated greater state control over the oil industry.[17]

When the results of the election were declared, the PNM had won a majority of the seats. Of the 24 elective seats contested, the PNM won 13 but with only 39 percent of the votes cast. The PDP won five seats with 20.3 percent of the votes. The TLP and the Butler Party each won two seats, and the remaining two seats were won by independents. The POPPG failed to win any seats in the legislature. The party performed well in areas where whites predominated, but these were not enough to earn the party a seat. The PNM won its seats from the predominantly black urban areas. It failed to win any seats in areas in which Indians predominated, especially in the sugar belt. In these areas, the PDP was triumphant. In fact, the PDP fielded candidates in only 14 of the 24 constituencies. It did not put up candidates in any of the areas where the blacks had a majority, such as San Fernando, Port-of-Spain, and Laventille.[18] Thus while a two-party system seemed to have emerged, its basis was ethnic. This became even more evident after the federal elections of 1958.

THE FEDERAL ELECTIONS

A federation of the British West Indian islands had been proposed by the British government as the price for independence from Britain. Trinidad was one of the ten colonies that opted to join the federation. Port-of-Spain, Trinidad, was chosen as the federal capital. The West Indies Federation came into effect in January 1958, and elections for the federal parliament were scheduled for April of that year.[19]

Two federal parties contested the election. The first was the Federal Labor Party led by Norman Manley of Jamaica. Manley had successfully persuaded the PNM to join his federal party, so that the PNM became the Trinidad unit of the Federal Labor Party. The other federal party was the Democratic Labor Party led by Sir Alexander Bustamante, Manley's cousin and political rival. In an effort to establish a Trinidad unit of the federal Democratic Labor Party, Bustamante visited Trinidad on May 17, 1957, and held discussions on the subject with the executives of the PDP, the TLP, the POPPG, and the Butler Party. Of these parties, the PDP, the TLP and the POPPG agreed to become affiliated to the federal Democratic Labor Party. In fact, on May 23, 1957, the Trinidad unit of the Democratic Labor Party was launched, which was no more than a loose coalition of the PDP, TLP, and the POPPG. However, the leaders of these three parties realized that it made little sense to unite in federal politics and yet oppose each other in local politics. At a special conference of the three parties held on July 18, 1957, a decision was taken to dissolve the three parties and to form a single party to be called the Democratic Labor Party (DLP) of Trinidad and Tobago; this party would also serve as the Trinidad affiliate of the federal Democratic Labor Party. The leader of Trinidad's DLP was Bhadase Sagan Maraj, and the DLP became the official opposition in the Legislative Council of Trinidad.[20]

The Federal Labor Party, to which the PNM was affiliated, portrayed itself as a socialist united front. The DLP of Trinidad, on the other hand, campaigned against the establishment of any form of socialism in the West Indies. The deputy leader of the party, Ashford Sinanan, stated: "We are inflexible in our advocacy at all times that the only hope of the entire West Indies is the belief in private enterprise."[21]

The results of the 1958 elections shocked Williams and the PNM. The DLP defeated the PNM by winning six out of the ten federal seats allocated to Trinidad. It was clear that the victory of the DLP was made possible by the support of non-Indian groups, including blacks, who were disenchanted with Williams and the PNM. Williams made his reaction to this defeat known a few days after the elections. In an address before a predominantly black audience, Williams accused the Indian community of voting on the basis of race. He also chastised the black population for apathy and lethargy and for not rallying around the PNM. Williams was criticized for this speech by the press and political opposition because it seemed to lay the foundation for further ethnic polarization in the colony.[22] Thus participation in the federal election of 1958 had the effect of entrenching a two-party system in Trinidad, but it also had the effect of intensifying racial animosity on the island.

LEADERSHIP PROBLEMS WITHIN THE DLP

The DLP had been established by a coalition of three political parties, united in their opposition to the PNM. Its leader, Bhadase Sagan Maraj, was very successful not only in mobilizing the support of the Indians, but also in manipulating the discontented non-Indian elements in the country. The results of the 1958 federal elections had demonstrated this. However, the younger Indians within the party were unhappy with Maraj's leadership. They felt that he lacked education, that his manners and methods were crude, and that he was no intellectual match for Williams. They wished to see Maraj replaced by someone of the intellectual stature of Williams.

In 1959, an opportunity for a change in leadership arose when Maraj was kept out of active politics by protracted illness. Because no one seemed capable of maintaining discipline within its ranks, the party was in disarray. The search for another leader intensified and the choice eventually fell on Dr. Rudranath N. Capildeo.

Rudranath Capildeo had had a brilliant academic career. He had earned his Ph.D. in physics from London University. During 1958-59, he was the principal of Trinidad Polytechnic and was therefore available locally. Those who supported his candidacy for the party leadership felt that such a move would enable the DLP to woo back Indian intellectuals and professionals, provide a hero figure for the rural Indian masses, and at the same time attract the non-Indians who were alienated from the PNM with a candidate of intellectual caliber. Although the selection was accompanied by bitter factional struggles, the fear of another five years of black rule if the PNM prevailed in the forthcoming elections forced a closing of ranks behind the new leader.[23] However, as events would reveal, Capildeo was ineffectual as a politician.

The 1961 election was held amidst intense racial lobbying and charges by the opposition that the new electoral rules had been formulated to disadvantage them. As a former DLP official pointed out, all previous elections had been "ballot box" elections, including the 1958 federal elections, which the PNM lost. The PNM government proposed to introduce voting machines in the 1961 election. The DLP objected to this change on two grounds. First, the DLP argued that the voting machines would scare away many unsophisticated rural voters. Second, the DLP voiced the suspicion that the voting machines had been fixed to ensure a PNM victory. They challenged the government to have the machines independently examined and suggested that the machines be used on an experimental basis in the local government elections prior to the 1961 national election. The PNM government refused.

The DLP also objected to the manner in which voter registration was conducted as well as to the way in which the electoral boundaries were demarcated. The DLP argued that too many powers were granted to the registration officers, who were predominantly blacks and therefore assumed to be pro-PNM, and that it did not expect free and impartial registration of voters, given the state of race relations in the country. The DLP also expressed its fears about the fairness of electoral boundaries which were to be demarcated by a PNM-dominated commission. Of these boundaries, Selwyn Ryan had this to say: "There is no doubt whatsoever in the writer's mind that the constituencies were gerrymandered."[24] The PNM used the results of the 1958 federal election in the demarcation of new electoral boundaries. The idea was to group large numbers of Indians into one constituency where possible, and to subdivide other Indian communities and attach the subdivisions to constituencies with large concentrations of blacks.

Racial tempers flared in this election. As Yogendra Malik states, "Programme and policy were secondary questions in the election of 1961: it was primarily a struggle between the two ethnic groups for political power."[25] In a campaign speech, Eric Williams suggested that a black who did not identify with the PNM was a traitor. Capildeo, who was provoked by the heckling and stone-throwing by PNM supporters, issued a call to arms. He told his supporters to "arm yourselves with weapons in order to take over this country."[26] This appeal to violence alienated many of his middle-class supporters. It also provided the PNM with an excuse to declare a state of emergency in areas of DLP support, where the police also conducted searches for arms. It was in this heated atmosphere that elections were held. When the results of the election were declared, the PNM had won 20 of the 30 seats with 57 percent of the popular vote, and the DLP won the remaining 10 seats with 42 percent of the vote.[27]

Williams had won another term in office. In fact, he was never defeated at the polls. Opponents claimed that he maintained political power by subtly manipulating racial sentiments within the country. He used the threat of domination by non-black groups to forge cohesion within the black majority. He also used his control over the state machinery to dispense patronage. He created a massive "special works" program (see Chapter 3).

Opposition leaders charged that Williams bought over all of the public utilities in the 1960s and turned these into employment agencies for party members. He also manipulated the electoral boundaries. According to opposition leaders interviewed by the author in 1982, these continued to be the means utilized by the PNM to maintain itself in office after Williams' death in 1981.

FRAGMENTATION OF THE DLP

On August 31, 1962, Trinidad became independent, and the PNM settled into the remaining four years of its rule. Within the DLP, however, a system of absentee leadership began to develop. Capildeo, the DLP leader, accepted a teaching position at the University of London in 1963. However, Capildeo retained the leadership position in the DLP, as well as in the parliamentary opposition. He only attended a few sittings of this entire legislative term and did so when the university recessed. This anomaly caused havoc within the DLP leadership. The POPPG and the TLP elements of the party broke away in 1964 and formed the Liberal Party under the leadership of Peter Farquhar. What remained of the DLP was essentially the Indian component of the party.

Further fragmentation followed within the Indian residue of the party. Capildeo had appointed Stephen Maharaj, a druggist, to act as the party leader during his absence. However, Maharaj could not exercise effective control over the party for two reasons. First, he did not have a high level of formal education. In fact, he compared poorly with the other senior party officials, who had high academic credentials and who challenged his leadership. Second, Maharaj was a socialist whereas the senior members of the executive had strong links with the business community.

The differences between Maharaj and the rest of the DLP executives took the form of an open confrontation in 1965. On March 12, 1965, the PNM government introduced a bill designed to restrict the ability of trade unions to strike. Maharaj issued instructions to the DLP parliamentarians to vote against the bill. However, not only did they defy his instructions and vote for the bill, they also engineered his dismissal as leader of the opposition. Maharaj then broke from the DLP and joined with several other prominent socialists to establish the Workers' and Farmers' Party.

The next split in the DLP came in 1968. Capildeo had returned to Trinidad to contest the 1966 election. The number of seats in the legislature had been increased from 24 to 36. The PNM won 24 of those seats and the DLP won the remaining 12. However, shortly after the elections, Capildeo went back to England, and Vernon Jamadar became the acting leader of the party. In 1968, the DLP executive delivered an ultimatum to Capildeo, requiring him either to return to Trinidad or relinquish the leadership of the party. Since Capildeo did not return, he was removed from the position of party leader. This provoked a further division of the DLP into two factions: a pro-Capildeo faction and a pro-Jamadar faction.

The *coup de grace* to Capildeo's political career was delivered by the speaker of the legislature in 1968 when he refused Capildeo any further leave of absence from the sessions of parliament and declared the seat vacant. A by-election was held in Capildeo's constituency of Chaguanas. It was won by Bhadase Sagan Maraj, who was attempting a political comeback. In January 1969, the pro-Capildeo faction in the legislature linked up with Bhadase Sagan Maraj. Bhadase Maraj called this group the Democratic Liberation Party, an obvious attempt to capitalize on the symbolic importance of the initials DLP.

In 1970, a split occurred in the PNM. The Deputy Prime Minister, A.N.R. Robinson, resigned from office. He later founded the Action Committee of Dedicated Citizens (ACDC). The ACDC formed a coalition with the Jamadar faction of the DLP in order to contest the 1971 elections. Robinson insisted on electoral reforms before he would contest the national elections. When such reforms were not forthcoming, the ACDC-DLP coalition ran a very strong campaign advocating a mass boycott of the election. It proved to be a very effective campaign even though the ACDC-DLP alliance was dissolved before the election. It was the lowest voter turnout in Trinidadian history. Only 33.6 percent of those eligible actually cast their votes. Also, as a result of the ACDC-DLP efforts, Bhadase Sagan Maraj's Democratic Liberation Party, which ran against the PNM and thereby legitimized the election, failed to win any seats. The PNM thus won all 36 seats with 28.3 percent of the vote.[28]

In the latter part of 1972, there was a thrust within the DLP (Jamadar) to initiate unity talks with the Democratic Liberation Party. Both Rudranath Capildeo and Bhadase Sagan Maraj had died, and it was felt by some that rapprochement was possible. Jamadar apparently opposed the move and it fell through. This precipitated a further split in the Democratic Labor Party. At a special convention of the party held on December 3, 1972, Jamadar and two of his lieutenants were removed from their positions within the party. Party leadership was passed on to Alloy Lequay, the party's general secretary. Jamadar responded by taking the matter to the High Court to get an annulment of the special convention and its proceedings. The matter dragged on in the courts for about two years. In November 1974, the High Court ruled against the Jamadar motion. Jamadar appealed the court's decision, but lost the appeal.[29]

The final blow to the Democratic Labor Party came in the 1976 general election. Two factions of the party contested the election, one faction under Jamadar and the other under Lequay. Neither won any seats, and the party--all factions of it--seems to have disappeared from the political scene.

ETHNICITY AND PUBLIC POLICY

The ethnic basis of politics in Trinidad relegated all other issues or policies to a secondary position. Ethnicity guaranteed the PNM an uninterrupted tenure in office between 1956 and 1986. The ethnic arithmetic ensured that the governing party would not be penalized electorally for its policies, including those affecting the oil and sugar industries, the principal pillars of the Trinidadian economy. However, security of tenure bred complacency on the part of the government. Until 1969, when it was jolted by the impending withdrawal of British Petroleum, the government had instituted no new petroleum policy.

The parliamentary opposition party, the DLP, did not make any significant impact on policymaking in general, and on oil policy in particular. The DLP drew its support predominantly from the East Indian population, the bulk of whom resided in the sugar belt. Not surprisingly, the sugar industry became the principal concern of the DLP. It is questionable whether the DLP or its affiliated union advanced the interests of the sugar workers as much as it could, but the party developed a competence in the sugar industry which it did not develop in the oil industry. It could be argued that given the ethnic voting pattern and the fact that the oil belt was populated largely by blacks, the DLP may not have been as motivated to take as close an interest in the oil industry as it did in the sugar industry. However, as the national opposition party, the DLP failed to take advantage of its position to question or initiate changes in oil policy. Consequently, the PNM government was relieved of an important source of domestic pressure to re-examine its oil policy.

Further, while the PNM was consolidating its hold on the government, the parliamentary opposition became caught in internal turmoil and fragmentation. First, the DLP leader tried to run the affairs of the party from London. This set in motion a struggle for the leadership of the party. Then, of course, factional strife drove the party out of existence. The organizational troubles that plagued the party consumed the energies and abilities of its leaders and gave the PNM a free hand in the running of the government. In the oil industry, this translated into a continuation of colonial policy and relative freedom of operation for the multinationals.

However, the fragmentation of the DLP created a political vacuum which the radical unions, led by the oil union, began to fill. The oil union leadership and its political allies realized that any serious challenger to the PNM had to be able to bridge the ethnic gap between the blacks and the Indians. Eventually they chose the issue of foreign control over the key sectors of the economy in order to mobilize cross-racial opposition to the PNM government.

NOTES

1. Opposition leaders who were interviewed in 1982 complained that the PNM government engaged in massive gerrymandering of the constituencies. They claimed that the Electoral District Boundaries Commission was usually packed with PNM supporters and that the Commission tried to create majorities for the PNM in most constituencies by using the results of previous elections.

2. Selwyn D. Ryan, Race and Nationalism in Trinidad and Tobago: A Study of Decolonization in a Multiracial Society (Toronto: University of Toronto Press, 1972), pp. 28-37. See also Ivar Oxaal, Black Intellectuals Come to Power: The Rise of Creole Nationalism in Trinidad and Tobago (Cambridge, Mass.: Schenkman Publishing Company, 1968), pp. 50-51.

3. Ryan, Race and Nationalism, pp. 39-41.

4. Ibid., pp. 45-46.

5. Ibid., pp. 58-67. See also the OWTU pamphlet, Oilfields Workers' Trade Union, July 1937-July 1977 (Trinidad and Tobago: Syncreators Ltd., 1977), p. 19.

6. Yogendra K. Malik, East Indians in Trinidad: A Study in Minority Politics (London: Oxford University Press, 1971), p. 76.

7. Ann Spackman, "Constitutional Development in Trinidad and Tobago," Social and Economic Studies 14 (December 1965), pp. 285-287.

8. Ryan, Race and Nationalism, pp. 86-90.

9. Spackman, "Constitutional Development in Trinidad and Tobago," p. 288.

10. For Williams' own account of his relations with the Caribbean Commission and his entry into politics, see Eric E. Williams, Inward Hunger: The Education of a Prime Minister (London: Andre Deutsch, 1969), pp. 81-143.

11. Ryan, Race and Nationalism, p. 109.

12. Oxaal, Black Intellectuals Come to Power, p. 100.

13. Ibid., p. 101.

14. Ryan, Race and Nationalism, p. 103.

15. Malik, East Indians in Trinidad, pp. 92-93.

16. Ibid., pp. 83-87.

17. Ryan, Race and Nationalism, pp. 128-138.

18. Malik, East Indians in Trinidad, pp. 94-95.

19. Ibid., p. 96.

20. Ibid., pp. 97-99.

21. Ryan, Race and Nationalism, p. 187.

22. Ibid., pp. 187-195.

23. Malik, East Indians in Trinidad, pp. 106-107.

24. Ryan, Race and Nationalism, p. 245, footnote 14.

25. Malik, East Indians in Trinidad, pp. 112- 113.

26. Ryan, Race and Nationalism, p. 268.

27. Malik, East Indians in Trinidad, p. 120.

28. Ryan, Race and Nationalism, pp. 482-483.

29. Interview with author, San Fernando, Trinidad, March 23, 1982. See also Alloy Lequay's personal account of the final year of the DLP in "Democratic Labor Party: The Struggle for Unity, 1968-1975" (undated).

5 NATIONALIZATION AS A MOBILIZATION STRATEGY

After the 1961 elections, ethnicity became the dominant variable of political life in Trinidad. The PNM came to be identified as the defender of black interests in the country, and the DLP, at least up until 1966, came to be identified with the interests of the East Indian community. It became clear to the Trinidadian left[1] that in order to challenge the PNM government, it needed the support of the East Indians. The strategy adopted by the political left to forge an inter-ethnic alliance between the blacks in the oil belt and the East Indians in the sugar belt was to appeal to the common class interests of both groups. Essential to this strategy was the identification of the foreign capitalists in the oil and sugar industries as the common enemy of the working class. Thus the demand for the nationalization of the oil and sugar companies, while consistent with the socialist beliefs of its advocates, was an essential part of a mobilization strategy aimed at unseating the PNM from political office. What is noteworthy is the role that trade unions played in the mobilization effort.

Trade unions in Trinidad had carved out a political role for themselves long before the country became independent. Since its founding, the Oilfields Workers' Trade Union (OWTU) has favored a socialist approach to development, and has tried to make common cause with the rural proletariat in the sugar industry. The first post-independence attempt to forge a coalition between black oil workers and Indian sugar workers took place in 1965. The PNM government prevented its consummation by declaring a state of emergency and by enacting a law to proscribe strikes.

A second attempt to unite the oil and sugar workers was made during the Black Power revolution of 1969-1970. Although the revolt failed to bring down the government, it marked a significant turning point in domestic politics. The role of the foreign companies in the economy of the country became firmly established as a major issue of domestic politics. When fragmentation of the DLP rendered that organization politically ineffective, radical unions rushed in to fill the political vacuum. Between 1974 and 1977, the political left intensified its efforts to forge an inter-ethnic alliance by using the demand for the nationalization of the foreign oil and sugar companies, which were portrayed as exploiters of the black and Indian working classes. A coalition developed but parochial interests and ideological differences caused the coalition to fragment.

THE GENESIS OF POLITICAL UNIONISM IN TRINIDAD

The major unions in Trinidad predate all of the current political parties.[2] In fact, before 1956, political parties were very weak. In the 1950 election, for example, 141 candidates, most of whom were independents, contested for the 18 available seats in the legislature. In this setting, trade unions took on political functions.

The labor movement had played a major role in advancing Trinidad toward self-government. It had fought for constitutional reform in the colony. It was the 1937 strike, organized by Butler and Rienzi, that had forced the British authorities to consider constitutional changes that would allow more mass political participation.

The growth of the trade union movement accelerated after the 1937 strike. Soon after the strike, several unions became registered, including the Oilfields Workers' Trade Union (OWTU), the All-Trinidad Sugar Estates and Factory Workers' Trade Union (ATSEFWTU), the Federated Workers' Trade Union (FWTU), and the Seamen and Waterfront Workers' Trade Union (SWWTU).[3]

The British authorities embarked on a concerted effort to wean these multiplying trade unions away from political activities and to cultivate industrial trade unions patterned after those existing in Britain. In February 1938, George Lindon, a British trade unionist, was sent to Trinidad in an official capacity as industrial adviser. Lindon was followed by other British labor experts over the years. The presence of these metropolitan labor experts helped to increase the tolerance of employers to the new unions and actually contributed to the speedy recognition of several of these.[4] However, these labor experts failed to achieve their principal goal, which was the establishment of a tradition of business unionism. Political unionism thrives in Trinidad.

At a very early stage, there developed within the trade union movement the view that political power was a prerequisite for the economic emancipation of the worker. The Oilfields Workers' Trade Union seemed to be the most vocal on this score. John Rojas of the OWTU stated that

> The struggle against capitalist exploitation is necessarily a political struggle. The working class cannot develop its economic organization and wage its economic battles without political rights, and without first coming into political power."[5]

In 1946, the Oilfields Workers' Trade Union, the Federated Workers' Trade Union, and the Southern Workers' Trade Union contested the national election under the banner of the Trades Union Council and Socialist Party, and won two of the nine available seats. The party had advocated the nationalization of the oil industry.[6]

In the 1956 election, several trade union leaders formed the Caribbean National Labor Party (CNLP) and contested the election. The leader of the CNLP was John Rojas, who was then the president-general of the OWTU. In a departure from the 1946 election platform, Rojas did not advocate the complete nationalization of the oil industry, but rather that the government of Trinidad should buy into those foreign oil companies that wished to sell their holdings. It is interesting to note that in this election, the CNLP failed to win any seats in parliament. But more importantly, although John Rojas was the head of the Oilfields Workers' Trade Union as well as of the CNLP, the party failed to win any of the seats in the oil belt. However, the view that political power was a prerequisite for the economic advancement of the workers would persist among some unions led by the OWTU.

PNM COURTSHIP OF ORGANIZED LABOR

As has been pointed out in the previous chapter, the PNM had been very shaken by its electoral defeat in the 1958 federal elections. Recalling that the party had been opposed by a significant segment of labor in the 1956 election and that it had failed to win any of the seats in the oil belt where the blacks predominated, the PNM's 1961 election appeal to these potential supporters was two-pronged. The first strategy has been recounted in Chapter 4 and involved an appeal to ethnicity, although this strategy was by no means confined to the PNM. In fact, the 1961 election has been portrayed in the literature as a racial confrontation.[7] An ethnic appeal to the blacks was also certain to penetrate organized labor where the black presence was predominant. In this effort, the PNM was very successful. As one opposition political leader explained, "Because the urban unions have tended to mobilize mostly Negro workers, the PNM posing as a defender of the blacks was able to win their support."[8] However, the PNM took no chances and their second strategy was to woo the support of organized labor as a group.

In a pre-election speech, Williams stated:

> If there is any group in the community which is going to defend democracy and self-government, that group is the workers. . . if any group is the repository of patriotism, that would be the workers of the country. No government will survive without the point of view of the labor movement behind it. . . . After the elections I recognize my friends.[9]

This speech served as a boost to the activities of the labor movement. However, given the type of development strategy adopted by the PNM, a collision with labor groups was inevitable. But for the moment, re-election into office was the preeminent concern of the PNM.

While the PNM was making overtures to the labor movement, the opposition DLP seemed to be alienating organized labor by its pronouncements. In its party organ The Statesman, the DLP took note of the state of industrial unrest prevailing in the country and advocated governmental action to curb it. Capildeo, the party leader, spoke out against labor strikes, warning that they would discourage foreign investment. He accused the PNM of using the trade unions to serve political ends and advocated the separation of trade unionism from party politics.[10]

The pronouncements of DLP politicians on labor issues, particularly the call by the party for governmental action to curb labor unrest in the country, drew condemnation from the labor movement. Carl Tull, then secretary-general of the National Trade Union Congress (NTUC), the umbrella organization of Trinidadian trade unions, saw the DLP position as a threat to the trade union and condemned the DLP leader for his stand on labor strikes. John Rojas, president of the NTUC, accused the DLP of being a conservative party supported by big business, despite the fact that it had a labor name. The leaders of the NTUC pledged the support of their organization to the PNM and decided to back this pledge by mass demonstrations in favor of the PNM. The Indian members of the National Trade Union Council, as well as a segment of Oilfields Workers' Trade Union, dissociated themselves from these activities and condemned the decision of the NTUC to support the PNM.[11]

The NTUC organized mass demonstrations in the major towns in support of the PNM. These were noisy and often disorderly. Both the Trinidad Guardian and the DLP called on the government to ban the marches. Williams' reply was that the Guardian enjoyed the freedom of the press and that the workers had the right of assembly. To the supporting trade unions, Williams declared, "March where the hell you like."[12]

The labor demonstrations and parades in support of the PNM led to an outbreak of violence in the vicinity of Port-of-Spain. In the towns of San Juan, Barataria, and St. Augustine, the DLP offices and homes of party candidates and supporters were stoned. The PNM government declared a state of emergency in these areas and later extended it to include the electoral districts of Caroni East and Chaguanas, which were all heavily populated by DLP supporters. House-to-house searches for arms and ammunition, conducted by the police, failed to uncover anything illegal. These actions were all condemned by the DLP as an attempt to intimidate its supporters.[13]

The results of the 1961 election gave the PNM a majority in the legislature. It is important to note here that the PNM won the seats in the oil belt. The results of the election convinced the Indian leaders that based on the racial arithmetic, the PNM would continue to win national elections, and that for the DLP to secure the interests of its constituents, it should shift its position from confrontation to cooperation with the PNM. Moreover, given the PNM's emphasis on foreign investment for the development of Trinidad and the DLP's support for private investment in general, there was very little ideological difference between the two parties. Williams too must have recognized that the DLP could no longer successfully challenge him at the polls. He welcomed the cooperation of the DLP and later used many opposition members to perform state functions. On the other hand, Williams recognized that the threat to the successful implementation of his development plan lay in the labor movement and soon turned to face it.

THE INDUSTRIALIZATION EFFORT

When the PNM took office in 1956, the oil and sugar industries dominated the economy. As in other developing countries, the government embarked on a program to diversify the economy by expanding the manufacturing sector. The program was called "industrialization by invitation," and a pivotal role was earmarked for foreign investment. The program was based on an economic blueprint drawn up for the West Indies by the economist W.A. Lewis.[14] It recognized the small size of islands such as Trinidad, their limited resource bases, their small domestic markets, and paucity of both domestic capital and technological expertise. The way to develop the manufacturing sector was to create the conditions that would attract foreign investment. Foreign enterprise would bring into the country the requisite capital, technology, organizational structure, and access to metropolitan markets. The incentives that would be provided to these foreign investors included tax holidays, duty rebates on imports of machinery, equipment, and raw materials, accelerated depreciation allowances, and cheap access to industrial sites with adequate infrastructural preparation. In return, governments could expect that local raw materials would be used, local employment and income would be generated, and foreign exchange would be earned. Further, the goal of diversification of the economy would be achieved and the traditional dependence on a single product reduced.

The program of "industrialization by invitation" had been set in motion prior to the accession of the PNM government. In 1950, the Aid to Pioneer Industries Ordinance was passed, in which an incentive structure was provided to new investors. A pioneer industry was defined to be any manufacturing industry that was not being conducted in Trinidad at all or not on a commercial scale. Four principal types of concessions were embodied in the ordinance. Imports of buildings materials, tools, plant machinery, and other appliances and materials necessary to ensure the final availability of the pioneer product were exempted from duty. Second, the pioneer manufacturer enjoyed a tax holiday of five years, with the possibility of an extension for a further period of up to five years. Third, the industry was granted allowances for accelerated depreciation on plant and equipment, and also for scientific research. These allowances took effect after the tax holiday ended. Finally, the manufacturer was assured that losses incurred during a tax holiday could be offset against income arising in the period immediately following the tax holiday period.[15]

In addition, arrangements were made for the avoidance and relief of double taxation with the United States, the United Kingdom, Canada, New Zealand, and most of the British Commonwealth countries. Further, income tax relief was provided to certain industries that could not qualify for pioneer status. The privileges of accelerated depreciation were extended to selected industries which included the sugar and oil industries.[16] The PNM government accepted the logic of the Lewis formula and proceeded to implement it.

However, what was lacking in the implementation was the acquiescence of labor. The program relied on cheap and docile labor. The government advertised the cheapness of labor to foreign enterprise. The general level of wages in Trinidad, it pointed out, was one-third that prevailing in the United States and one-half that in the United Kingdom.[17] However, the government in these early years outlined no program to keep wage levels low. Given the great emphasis it placed on foreign investment, a confrontation with organized labor seemed inevitable.

Table 5.1 Industrial Disputes Involving Stoppages of Work, 1950-1964

YEAR	NUMBER OF WORK STOPPAGES	NUMBER OF WORKDAYS LOST
1950	16	NA
1951	13	NA
1952	5	NA
1953	7	49,157
1954	5	NA
1955	3	20,660
1956	7	213,930
1957	6	3,112
1958	7	13,968
1959	69	23,383
1960	31	275,223
1961	35	145,105
1962	75	164,659
1963	48	204,971
1964	44	95,906

Source: The Central Statistical Office, <u>Annual Statistical Digest 1959</u> and <u>Annual Statistical Digest 1966</u>.

THE LABOR SITUATION IN THE EARLY 1960S

Well before the 1961 election campaign got underway, it was clear that labor strikes were on the increase. As Table 5.1 shows, there was a disproportionate increase in the number of strikes in 1959 as compared to previous years. And while the number of strikes fell in 1960 and 1961, in terms of number of workdays lost, these strikes were longer and costlier. Williams' open sponsorship of trade union activities during his 1961 election campaign gave impetus to increased labor agitation. As Table 5.1 shows, the number of strikes in 1962 more than doubled that of the previous two years. In 1963 and 1964, the frequency of strikes remained fairly high. The principal reasons for the strikes were wages and conditions of work, union recognition, and disputes arising from dismissals and suspensions. The question of union recognition involved a great amount of poaching by some unions. It was becoming easy, in the absence of any legal restraints, for a strong union in one industry to gobble up a weaker union in another industry if it could set up a foothold there. Intra-union conflicts were also frequent and intense, and employers attempted to influence the outcomes of these struggles. Strike action was one way a faction could establish its strength and justify its claim to leadership of the union.[18]

The high level of industrial unrest posed a serious threat to the government's industrialization plan, a plan that depended on foreign investment. So far, the government had played the role of bystander while the various industrial disputes raged. It was now determined to change its position, and the oil union provided a useful opening.

The oil union was one of the unions with a serious internal struggle for leadership. Since the late 1950s, a rebel group within the union had been challenging the leadership of president John Rojas. In the 1961 national election, John Rojas campaigned actively in the oil belt for the PNM. After the election, the PNM rewarded Rojas by nominating him to be a senator. However, on March 27, 1962, the general council of the OWTU approved a motion of no confidence, passed at the Palo Seco branch, against the president of the union, John Rojas, and the general secretary, Joseph Houlder. In early April, Rojas resigned from the leadership of the OWTU, which he had held for 19 years. In his place, George Weekes, leader of the rebel group, became president of the union.[19]

Within a few months after his departure from the oil union, Rojas made some declarations that put the entire trade union movement, and particularly the OWTU, on the defensive. In a senate speech in August 1962, Rojas alleged Marxist infiltration of the trade union movement. Rojas went on to say that some of the most powerful unions in Trinidad were headed by Marxists. He claimed that these men were collaborating with others outside of the trade union movement to bring about a revolution in Trinidad.[20] The PNM reacted to this speech by instituting a commission of inquiry to investigate subversive activities in Trinidad.

Although the inquiry was aimed at the trade union movement and although the nature of the inquiry could potentially affect the reputation of the movement, the National Trade Union Council did not react in any united way. The NTUC did not issue any official objection to the inquiry, although individual unions questioned the need for such an inquiry and the areas of investigation. From the report of the commission of inquiry, it is clear that the focus of the investigation was the Oilfields Workers' Trade Union, its connection with other unions such as the Civil Service Association and the National Union of Government Employees, and with what the commission regarded as the only communist organization in the island, the West Indian Independence Party.

The West Indian Independence Party (WIIP) had been formed in 1952 under the leadership of Lennox Pierre. The party contested the 1956 election without gaining any seats or demonstrating any significant following. It was regarded as a communist party. It was in the leadership of the party that the commission of inquiry took particular interest. Among the party's first executive officers were John Rojas, president of the OWTU, and Quintin O'Connor, president of the Federated Workers' Trade Union. Under pressure from their respective unions, both men had withdrawn from the WIIP and formed the Caribbean National Labor Party (CNLP). After the 1956 election, the party membership dwindled, but a few hard-core members remained. Among them were Lennox Pierre and George Weekes, who later replaced Rojas as head of the OWTU. It was said that the WIIP was the political arm of the OWTU. It has also been part of the conventional wisdom in Trinidad that whoever controls the OWTU controls the economy of the country. This placed George Weekes, as head of the OWTU, in a preeminent position in the trade union movement, and the commission of inquiry examined the attempts by Weekes to increase his influence within the labor movement by promising strike action in the oil industry in support of the strikes of other unions such as the Civil Service Association and the National Union of Government Employees. The report of the commission was submitted to the governor-general of Trinidad in January 1964, but its presentation in parliament was held up until 1965 by court actions.[21]

The commission of inquiry regarded the West Indian Independence Party as a communist organization with strong influence in the trade union movement. The commission described George Weekes, president of the National Trade Union Congress and president of the Oilfields Workers' Trade Union, as a communist. While the commission found no evidence of any attempt to overthrow the government by violent means, it recommended increased vigilance on the part of the government. It also recommended that the government should observe closely the increased rate of strike action by unions with a view to setting up the machinery for its arrest.[22]

THE INDUSTRIAL STABILIZATION ACT

In 1965, a situation developed in the sugar industry that threatened the conservative leadership of the sugar union as well as the PNM government. The right of Bhadase Sagan Maraj to occupy the presidency of the union was being questioned. What made Maraj's position precarious was the fact that he had never been elected to that position. Krishna Gowandan, a young Indian Marxist who had developed a following within the union, challenged Maraj to face an election for the union's highest position. Gowandan's leadership bid had the support of some of the country's prominent Marxists, including George Weekes, president of the oil union and of the National Trade Union Congress; C.L.R. James, a prominent former member of the PNM; Stephen Maharaj, the acting leader of the DLP; and

Adrian Cola Rienzi, who was the only person to have occupied the presidency of the oil and sugar unions simultaneously and who continued to exercise considerable influence in both. These men saw an opportunity to integrate the new leaders of the sugar union into the leadership structure of the oil union. If the oil union could exercise a controlling influence over the sugar union, its stranglehold over the economy would be complete. Moreover, a coalition between the black oil workers and the Indian sugar workers would have enormous political importance. Such an ethnic alliance could alter the basis of future electoral victories.

In March 1965, a strike by thousands of sugar workers virtually closed down the sugar industry. Maraj tried in vain to break the strike by using substitute workers. The striking sugar workers invited George Weekes to speak to them. Weekes, who was also the president of the National Trade Union Congress, called an emergency meeting of the NTUC and succeeded in passing a resolution supporting the striking sugar workers. The NTUC also wrote to the government and the sugar company, Caroni Ltd., requesting a meeting to discuss the sugar strike with a view to finding some solution. The actions taken by the executive of the NTUC were opposed by other member unions. The Seamen and Waterfront Workers' Trade Union, of which Williams was the adviser, withdrew from the NTUC in protest.

Neither the sugar company nor the government responded to the NTUC request. Instead, the government, alarmed by the prospect of a link-up between the sugar and oil workers, hinted about a communist-inspired plot to create chaos in the country and declared a state of emergency in the sugar belt. Meetings and demonstrations were banned, movement of citizens within the area was restricted, and the police were authorized to conduct searches without warrants for explosives and subversive literature.[23]

A state of emergency was declared on March 18, 1965. Immediately afterwards, the Williams' government laid before parliament the report of the commission of inquiry into subversive activities in Trinidad. This was the first time that the contents of the report had been made public. It seems as if the timing of the presentation of this report was designed to create mass consternation and to justify the new restrictions that the government was about to impose on labor. On the same day, the Williams' government introduced and pushed through the legislature a bill designed to restrict the freedom of trade unions to strike. Apparently the Industrial Stabilization Act (ISA) had been in preparation for some time. Organizations like the NTUC that had a clear interest in the bill were not given any time to study it, though trade unionists connected with the PNM may have been consulted. In fact, in what has been described as an "amazing display of perverted class consciousness," several pro-government unions held demonstrations outside of parliament in support of the bill while it was being presented.[24]

In essence, the ISA proscribed the right to strike and introduced a system of compulsory arbitration in which the government would play a key role. The principal features of the ISA were as follows:

1. The ISA provided for the compulsory recognition of a union which enjoyed the support of more than 50 percent of the employees in the particular enterprise.

2.	It provided for the establishment of an industrial court with wide powers to settle industrial disputes, to register industrial agreements, and to settle disputes arising from these.

3.	The Act required that labor disputes be reported to the Minister of Labor for conciliation or for other steps to resolve them, including referring them to the industrial court.

4.	The Act stipulated a number of procedures that had to be followed before strike or lockout action could be taken. First, the dispute had to be reported to the Minister of Labor. If, however, the Minister referred the dispute to the industrial court within 28 days, strike or lockout action could not be taken. If, on the other hand, 28 days elapsed and the matter had not been referred to the industrial court, the party contemplating strike or lockout action had to give 14 days notice of the intended action.[25]

In effect, the ISA made the right to strike useless. It was clearly pro-business. Yet the government was able to marshal the support of several unions for this piece of legislation. It was steam-rollered through the legislature while a state of emergency existed in certain parts of the country and while the rest of the public was sifting through the report on subversive activities in the country. George Weekes, who had opposed the bill, resigned from his position as president of the National Trade Union Congress and took the oil union out of the NTUC from which it is still divorced.

Williams considered the ISA his outstanding achievement during his second term of office. He acknowledged that the act was aimed at preventing a link-up of the oil and sugar workers.[26] An alliance of the oil and sugar workers would have symbolized a breakdown of ethnic barriers. This naturally concerned Williams since ethnic polarization had worked to the advantage of the PNM in the previous elections. However, even if this alliance did not translate into votes against the PNM, control over the oil and sugar unions would have given the socialists de facto control over the country. By virtue of his control over the oil union, George Weekes already had control over the economy. If he could also exercise control over the second most powerful union and the second major industry in the country, he and the other socialists would be in a strategic position from which they could dictate terms to any government. Since these leaders favored a socialization of the economy, they could prod the government to nationalize the foreign companies in the oil and sugar industries. The ruling party was therefore determined to keep these two unions apart, and the instruments chosen for this purpose were a declaration of a state of emergency and the enactment of the ISA.

The socialists, on the other hand, never relinquished the goal of forging an alliance between the oil and sugar workers on the basis of common class interest. In fact, in 1966, George Weekes, along with Lennox Pierre, C.L.R. James, and some Indian Marxists--A.C. Rienzi, Stephen Maharaj, and a newcomer, Basdeo Panday--established the Workers' and Farmers' Party (WFP). The party contested the 1966 election with a multiracial slate of candidates. Yet in spite of the fact that the party had the confidence of the leadership of the oil union, the WFP failed to win even the seats in the oil belt. The PNM won 24 seats in the predominantly black areas, and the DLP won the remaining 12 in the predominantly Indian constituencies, an indication of strong ethnic voting and a reluctance on the part of the major ethnic groups to accommodate any party that could potentially split the vote that an ethnic majority could deliver in any constituency. However, the WFP leaders were not daunted by this experience.

THE BLACK POWER REVOLUTION

The first major challenge to the Industrial Stabilization Act came in May 1969 when the Transport and Industrial Workers' Union (TIWU) called a strike that brought the public transport system in Port-of-Spain to a halt. The strike received the active support of an impressive list of political and labor personalities. Seventeen people were arrested and charged with obstructing the free passage of buses out of the Port-of-Spain bus terminal. Among those arrested were Joseph Young, president of the transport union; George Weekes, president of the oil union and a member of the WFP; Stephen Maharaj, leader of the WFP; Lennox Pierre, legal adviser of the transport union and a member of the WFP; Peter Farquhar, leader of the Liberal Party; Basdeo Panday, editor of the OWTU's Vanguard and a member of the WFP; and Geddes Granger, a university student and chairman of the National Joint Action Council (NJAC).[27] The OWTU leadership promised to call out the oil workers for a two-hour solidarity strike.[28]

The TIWU strike marked the beginning of the breakdown of the ISA. According to a former minister of the PNM government, between 1969 and 1972, strikes and other infringements of the law made the ISA unenforceable. The government attempted some prosecutions but these proved to be ineffective in stopping the labor unrest.[29] Many of the strikes occurred in support of the so-called Black Power revolution.

In February and March of 1970, Trinidad was rocked by Black Power demonstrations in its major towns. The marches stressed themes of black dignity and called for the transfer of power into the hands of blacks. On the surface, these demands seemed ludicrous since the blacks were the majority in Trinidad and a black government was in power. However, the underlying causes of the demonstrations were economic.

The protests began in Trinidad in support of some West Indian students who alleged that they had been discriminated against on the basis of race by the authorities at the Sir George Williams University in Canada. Support for the students in Canada initially came from the National Joint Action Council, headed by Geddes Granger (now Makandal Daaga), the Student Guild of the St. Augustine campus of the University of the West Indies, of which Granger was the former president, and the National Freedom Movement. The protesters first marched to the Canadian High Commission, then to the Royal Bank of Canada, which some tried to enter. The protesters then temporarily occupied the Roman Catholic Cathedral of the Immaculate Conception on Independence Square. With these demonstrations, the issue of the students in Canada receded into the background. As Geddes Granger yelled to his followers: "Today we come here not so much to protest oppression against black people all over the world, but to protest the brutality against black people in Trinidad and Tobago."[30]

As a result of the demonstrations, several of the leaders, including Geddes Granger, were arrested and charged with unlawful assembly. The Oilfields Workers' Trade Union decided in an emergency meeting on February 28 to give moral and financial support to the arrested men. This was the beginning of the OWTU's public involvement with the Black Power movement. After a few days, the union threatened to call a general strike.[31]

On March 11, George Weekes called on the government to take over the sugar industry and run it in the national interest.[32] On March 23, in an address to Catholic teachers, Weekes called for the national ownership of the oil and sugar industries.[33] This call was repeated again in early April when Weekes told members of his union at Pointe-à-Pierre that the OWTU found itself in the ranks of the revolution. He said that the oil industry was a strong base of racialism against nationals, implying that oil workers were badly treated by white foreign managers. He insisted that something had to be done about this.[34]

On April 21, the government declared a state of emergency in the country. Shortly afterwards, the police arrested George Weekes, Winston Leonard, education officer of the OWTU, and several of the leaders of the various marches.[35] A few days later, Geddes Granger, who was being sought by the police, was arrested in San Fernando.

On April 23, news began to break of a mutiny within the army. After several days of negotiations with a team selected by the government, the leaders of the revolt surrendered. Three officers, Lt. Rex Lasalle, Lt. Rafique Shah, and Lt. Michael Barzey, were accused and tried for treason. The trials of those arrested continued for several months.[36]

The Black Power revolt is a very important landmark in Trinidad's history. It was the only time that the government was on the brink of violent overthrow. Though the dissident elements took on the Black Power label largely because of the manner in which the demonstrations began, the thrust of the protests was for economic improvement for urban blacks and for greater local control of the economy through local ownership of the oil and sugar industries. The oil union leadership was particularly vocal during this crisis in demanding the nationalization not only of the oil industry but also of the sugar industry. The demand for the nationalization of the sugar industry was used to mobilize the support and the active participation of the Indian population, and especially of the sugar workers. The attempt failed because Indian leaders interpreted the movement as anti-Indian, and the burning of Indian businesses served to confirm this.[37] The demonstrators were disaffected elements from the ranks of PNM supporters, and the ruling party could not completely ignore the demands.

By about the end of April 1970, the sting had been taken out of the Black Power movement. The government was in control again. However, it initiated some moves that were responsive to the demands of the Black Power militants. During the demonstrations, Williams had declared his sympathy for the demand that blacks exercise greater control over the economy. He announced that the government would nationalize the Bank of London and Montreal and establish it as a national bank. He also stated that the government would buy 51 percent of the ordinary stock of the country's largest sugar producer, Caroni Ltd., the Trinidadian subsidiary of the British firm, Tate and Lyle Ltd. Tate and Lyle would continue to run the company under a management contract. Williams emphasized that the purchase was aimed at achieving public participation, but not state ownership.[38] No similar plans were announced for existing oil companies.

The decision by the Williams' government to acquire equity ownership in the sugar industry is examined in greater detail later in this chapter. However, it should be noted here that the decision was part of the response to a domestic crisis in which the principal demand was for greater national control over the entire economy.

THE INDUSTRIAL RELATIONS ACT

It was clear after the Black Power demonstrations and the accompanying strikes that the ISA had not taken the teeth out of labor. In fact, the radical unions seemed to be gaining the upper hand. The OWTU, in 1969, had displaced an established union to become the bargaining representative of the workers in the Trinidad and Tobago Electricity Corporation (TTEC), a very strategic state corporation because of its sole handling of electricity generation, transmission, and distribution in the entire country.[39] Further, by mid-1972, it seemed as though the OWTU was making inroads insofar as representation of the water and sewage workers, telephone company, and dock workers were concerned. Each of these categories of workers already had a recognized union. However, the workers probably felt that they would be much better off economically if they were represented by the OWTU, which had a reputation as the most powerful union in the country. The OWTU no doubt made use of this reputation to further increase its strength.

The Trade Union Congress responded to these developments by issuing a statement accusing the OWTU of poaching in the jurisdictional areas of some of its affiliates. And the leadership of the Seamen and Waterfront Workers' Trade Union (SWWTU) issued an ultimatum warning that unless the OWTU stopped recruiting dock workers, the SWWTU would call out all of its workers on strike.[40] Since Trinidad has always been highly dependent on food imports, the SWWTU, by its control over the workers involved in port operations, has always occupied a strategic bargaining position. The threat of a strike by this union brought forth swift action by the government.

The government, pleading that a crisis in industrial relations existed, declared a state of emergency. It imprisoned several top-ranking officials of the OWTU, including the president, George Weekes. With the state of emergency in force, the government enacted the Industrial Relations Act (IRA), which updated and strengthened the ISA.[41] The industrial court was retained as the centerpiece of the industrial relations system. While strikes and lockouts are still possible, they can only occur if the Minister of Labor permits them, since referral of a dispute by him to the industrial court automatically prevents a strike or lockout.[42] Further, the ISA had listed certain "essential services" such as the security forces, health services, and fire services, in which strike action was forbidden. The IRA now added a list of "essential industries" to include: the electricity, water and sewage, fire, health, hospital, and sanitation services, the oil, gas, and petrochemical industries, the port operations, the sugar industry, the communications service, and the public bus transport service. A union representing workers in any one of these "essential industries" was restrained from also representing workers in any other essential industry, unless such was the case before the Act was promulgated.[43] This provision was aimed at checking the expansion of the OWTU.

The IRA strengthened the legal machinery initially set up by the ISA to handle labor issues. Trade union activities are restricted to purely industrial matters. The right to strike has been severely curtailed. The law also addresses the issue of trade union expansion. The restrictions governing union expansion into "essential industries" were motivated by a desire on the part of the PNM government to curb the ability of the OWTU to increase its strength by displacing weaker unions in the non-petroleum sectors. However, it was not long before the government was on the defensive again.

THE UNITED FRONT AGAINST THE MULTINATIONALS

The 1970 Black Power demonstrations had proven that economic nationalism had seeped into the broader society. It had even penetrated the ranks of the PNM. It showed that the strategy of utilizing the foreign companies as an issue for domestic political mobilization held tremendous promise. The OPEC price increases in 1973 gave the foreign oil companies in Trinidad increased visibility and made them an even more lucrative political target. By this time there had also been a change in the leadership of the sugar union. The new leadership favored the nationalization of the sugar industry. The stage was now set for an alliance between the oil workers' union and the sugar workers' union. The basis of this alliance would be the common call for the nationalization of foreign enterprise.

On November 4, 1974, the OWTU began negotiations with Texaco for a new collective agreement. The OWTU initially demanded a wage increase of 80 percent but later increased this to 147 percent. The bargaining strategy of the OWTU was based on the assumption that the profits of the oil companies had escalated with the energy crisis. Texaco made a counter-offer of 30 percent, which the union refused. The matter was then taken to the industrial court for a decision.[44]

At about this time also, the All-Trinidad Sugar Estates and Factory Workers' Trade Union was seeking a 100 percent increase in wages for its members. The sugar union was now headed by Basdeo Panday, who had contested the 1966 election with the Workers' and Farmers' Party and who was a former legal counsel to the OWTU. Apart from this wage dispute in the sugar industry, a union recognition issue also arose. Until now, sugar cane farmers were represented by the Trinidad Island-Wide Cane Farmers' Association (TICFA). However, the leadership of TICFA became increasingly identified with the PNM and the sugar company. A new union, the Island-Wide Cane Farmers' Trade Union (ICFTU), emerged to challenge the TICFA for the representation of the sugar cane farmers. The new union was headed by Raffique Shah, a former army lieutenant who had been one of the leaders of the army mutiny of 1970.[45] Shah and Weekes had become acquainted during their imprisonment in 1970. Weekes and Panday had been members of the Workers' and Farmers' Party. These three union leaders decided to get together in order to press more forcefully their respective demands.[46]

On February 18, 1975, the sugar and oil unions organized a mass rally at Skinner Park in San Fernando. The rally was attended by over 20,000 workers from the oil and sugar industries. This meeting of predominantly Indian and black workers had great political significance since it presaged a merger of the major ethnic groups with class becoming the major political variable.

At this rally, the OWTU, both sugar unions, and the Transport and Industrial Workers' Union (TIWU) decided to form an alliance to provide "a United Front to the multinationals."[47] The alliance was called the United Labor Front (ULF). The unions passed resolutions calling for the nationalization of the oil and sugar multinationals. The motto adopted was "Tate and Lyle [the sugar company] and Texaco must go."[48]

By March 11, 1975, the sugar industry was at a standstill as the sugar union called out its workers on strike. On March 12, the OWTU called a strike against Texaco. In an effort to bring their demands to national attention and to pressure the oil and sugar companies, the ULF organized a march for "Peace, Bread, and Justice," from the OWTU headquarters in San Fernando to Port-of-Spain. The march took place on March 18, but soon after it had begun, it was broken up by the police, and the leaders were arrested.[49]

It was evident that the government was deeply troubled by the industrial unrest, but particularly by the alliance between the two major unions. The marchers had been brutally dispersed by the police. This brought forth strong condemnation from the Trinidadian press but momentarily assured the government that demonstrations of the intensity of those in 1970 would not recur. However, the government had to respond to the call for the nationalization of the sugar and the oil industries.

It is true that the unions were using the nationalization issue to draw adverse publicity to the companies and to pressure them to become more receptive to the union demands. This tactic had been used in the past. In this case, however, the government had reason for concern. The alliance between black oil workers and Indian sugar workers has always had political significance. Bridging the racial gap between these two groups had been the aspiration of every challenger to Williams and the PNM. What made the ULF particularly threatening was the fact that a political vacuum existed owing to the fragmentation of the DLP. There was no opposition in parliament, elections were due in 1976, and the ULF, though still an alliance of trade unions, was drawing impressive crowds to its meetings. Eventually, the government decided to tackle the sugar industry.

By March 31, 1975, the government had increased its ownership of the sugar company Caroni Ltd. from 51 percent to 55 percent.[50] However, the union leadership saw little utility in this marginal increase and was adamant about complete national ownership. The sugar industry was at that time the second largest employer in the country. It was the lifeline of the people of central Trinidad, as well as those of the near south. The industry was not performing well. In fact, the business editor of the Trinidad Guardian had described the sugar company as a "sickly company."[51] In an interview with the author, a senior official in the sugar union explained that the union leadership saw that the country was becoming wealthy as a result of rising oil prices and felt that the national wealth should be shared. They recognized that the industry would have to be subsidized and felt that the government had the wealth to do so. Further, because sugar has always been a very political commodity, the union leadership felt certain that the government could be pushed in this direction.[52]

For its part, the government has always been sensitive to the political nature of sugar production in Trinidad. It was aware that the sugar industry was failing and that Tate and Lyle, the minority shareholders of Caroni Ltd., would not be unwilling to sell out. Complete acquisition of the sugar industry would not, therefore, adversely affect the government's relationship with other foreign enterprises and would not endanger the image of the country as a host for foreign investment. The domestic political payoffs would be enormous. Ownership of the sugar industry would allow the government to boast of further advance in its plan to control the commanding heights of the economy. The government would be credited with removing the last conspicuous vestige of British colonial rule and with setting the stage for the dismantling of the plantation system. By acquiring ownership of the sugar industry, the government would also have driven a wedge between the leadership of the sugar union and that of the oil union.

The government, by subsidizing the sugar industry, would appear as the benefactor of the sugar workers and would set the stage for a more collaborative relationship between the government and the union. But subsidization of sugar would depend on continued revenues from oil. Put another way, given the poor performance of the sugar industry, its nationalization would accentuate the country's dependence on oil. It could therefore be expected that the sugar union would soften its support for the nationalization of the oil industry if this carried some risk of disrupting the windfall from oil that had been set in motion by the OPEC countries. Presumably, with this consideration in mind, the government bought the remaining shares of Caroni Ltd. that were held by Tate and Lyle.

THE ULF IN PARLIAMENT

In January 1976, the leaders of the United Labor Front decided to transform the labor alliance into a political party. The principal reason given for this move was that it was necessary to hold political power before the workers could have true economic emancipation. It was the argument that had been advanced in the past to justify the OWTU's involvement in politics. However, as one ULF leader explained, this time the brutality with which the ULF marchers were dispersed on "Bloody Tuesday" (March 18, 1975) helped the leadership in their attempt to persuade the workers that regardless of how strong they were in terms of numbers, they could very easily be crushed if they did not have political power.[53] The ULF contested the national election in September 1976 and won 10 of the 36 seats, with 24 of these going to the PNM led by Williams.

The Marxist orientation of the ULF presaged an ideological battle in parliament. Until 1971, the parliamentary opposition that the PNM faced had been conservative and generally supportive of the PNM's policies, especially with regard to foreign investment in the country. Between 1971 and 1976, the PNM had been unopposed in parliament. Now, for the first time, the PNM confronted a party that claimed to be organized on a class basis. Marxists who had been challenging Williams for about two decades were finally in parliament. George Weekes of the OWTU and Lennox Pierre of the WIIP were senators, and Raffique Shah, the former lieutenant and co-leader of the 1970 army mutiny, was a member of the House of Representatives. Without question, the ULF posed the most serious parliamentary challenge that the PNM had ever faced.

However, less than a year after the election, the removal of Basdeo Panday as leader of the ULF by the party's central executive was public confirmation that the party was undergoing serious factional squabbling. Before the end of 1977 Panday had been reinstated, but a split in the party rendered it ineffectual for the duration of this parliamentary term.

While the ULF had been carrying on its industrial fight for improved wages and working conditions in 1975, it had attracted many leftist extremists. When the decision was taken to make the ULF a political party, there was a strong feeling among the leadership that the party needed an ideology. The ideological issue was never settled. Some felt that the parliamentary route was bourgeois and that the real way to acquire power was through the use of violence. A pro-Maoist and a pro-Moscow faction developed.[54] Panday, who had not yet been involved in the initial phase, became the focus of party criticism when he declared that the foreign capitalists should be seen as the principal enemy, but that the workers should form an alliance with local capitalists. He also saw parliament as the arena in which the political struggle should be carried out. He was accused of being a reactionary, and the central committee of the party, which was dominated by ultra-leftist elements, voted to remove him from the leadership of the party. It is clear in hindsight that the central committee had miscalculated the strength of Panday's support. The ten seats which the ULF had won were located in the sugar belt, and as head of the sugar union, Panday was responsible for the party's success at the polls. In fact, Weekes and the leaders of the oil union had failed to win the seats in the oil belt. In the end, Panday and the moderates triumphed, but the party was badly divided.

By the end of 1977, the PNM was certain that the threat the ULF initially posed had been removed. As one PNM official pointed out, despite the ULF's emphasis on class, the party had only succeeded in winning the seats in the traditional DLP strongholds. The implication here is that ethnicity and not class determined the results of the 1976 elections and that the ULF was simply the DLP under a new name. Or, as one leader of the Trinidad and Tobago National Alliance put it, Basdeo Panday had become the new leader of the "tribe" (the Indians).[55]

In 1981, the ULF contested the national elections as part of a coalition of parties called the Trinidad and Tobago National Alliance (TTNA). The other Alliance partners were the Tapia party, headed by Lloyd Best, and the Democratic Action Congress (DAC), headed by A.N.R. Robinson. Both Best and Robinson are black. One TTNA leader explained that the TTNA was an ethnic alliance. He said that the ULF (1975-1977) "pretended that it was a class alliance," but in reality it was an alliance between one faction which had a large ethnic following (the Indians) and one which did not. He continued that in establishing the TTNA, the leaders of the individual parties made an honest admission that ethnicity was the dominant political variable and that the TTNA was an ethnic alliance. The hope was that the leaders would develop credibility with their respective ethnic groups and would demonstrate that the major ethnic groups could work together.[56] With this admission, it appeared as though party organization in Trinidad had turned full circle.

The TTNA contested the December 1981 election but failed to unseat the PNM. The party won the traditional DLP seats, a reflection of the popularity of Basdeo Panday and the ULF wing in the Indian areas. The Alliance also won the two seats in Tobago because of the DAC's popularity there. The PNM won the remaining seats and a new five-year term in office. The other major party that contested the election was the Organization for National Reconstruction (ONR), led by Karl Hudson-Phillips, a former attorney general in the PNM government. Although the ONR performed respectably in terms of the total vote, it failed to win any constituency.

In 1985, the TTNA and the ONR merged to form the National Alliance for Reconstruction (NAR). It chose the former DAC leader, A.N.R. Robinson, to head the new party. The NAR contested the December 1986 election and overwhelmingly defeated the PNM. The NAR won 33 of the seats with the PNM retaining the rest. The first change of government since 1956 took place in December 1986.

NATIONALIZATION AND MOBILIZATION

The strong ethnic voting pattern that emerged in the 1960s dictated that any serious challenger to the PNM had to be able to bridge the ethnic gap between the Indians and the blacks. This task was taken up by the radical unions led by the oil union. Trade unions in Trinidad, and especially the oil union, had a history of active involvement in politics, and when the fragmentation of the DLP created a political vacuum, the oil union and its socialist allies moved to fill it. Their first strategy was to replace the conservative leadership of the sugar union with a socialist group and then to try to forge an alliance between the sugar workers and the oil workers by appealing to their common class interests. This strategy was foiled by the government.

It was, however, the Black Power revolution that suggested the efficacy of using the demand for the nationalization of the foreign companies in the oil and sugar industries as a strategy of mobilization. Until this time, the OWTU had been the only organization that had consistently advocated the nationalization of the oil industry. The demand by the Black Power demonstrators for the nationalization of the oil and sugar industries showed that economic nationalism had seeped into the wider society. The role of the foreign companies in the national economy had become an issue of domestic politics. The demand for nationalization of the foreign companies in the oil and sugar industries was now also being used as a strategy of mobilization.

This strategy was repeated during the period 1974 to 1977, when the international climate seemed propitious for nationalization and when high oil prices had enhanced the capacity of the government to undertake such action. The socialists portrayed the foreign companies in the oil and sugar industries as the common exploiters of the black workers in the oil industry and the Indian workers in the sugar industry. The strategy was successful in forging an alliance between these two groups of workers. This was symbolized by the ULF. However, not long after its founding, the ULF became torn by ideological differences, and the intensity of the nationalization demand subsided.

It was not simply the ideological differences within the ULF that accounted for the demise of nationalization as an issue of domestic politics. The policies pursued by the PNM government toward the multinationals were also a major contributing factor.

NOTES

1. The Trinidadian left consists of the radical trade unions within the Conference of Progressive Trade Unions (CPTU), intellectuals located at the St. Augustine campus of the University of the West Indies, and several micro-groups such as the United National Independence Party (UNIP), and the National Movement for the True Independence of Trinidad and Tobago (NAMOTI), which have very little, if any, support within the population. Here we are specifically referring to those who were closely identified with the Workers' and Farmers' Party in 1966.

2. This study employs Caswell Johnson's definition of political unionism:

> Political unionism . . . is said to exist if there is any systematic commitment among trade unions to mobilize votes and/or provide financial assistance for (or against) one or more political parties in exchange for some control over economic and social policy; or, if the trade union movement's social and political aspirations compete effectively with those of any political party for political support.

See Caswell L. Johnson, "Political Unionism and the Collective Objective in Economies of British Colonial Origin: The Cases of Jamaica and Trinidad," American Journal of Economics and Sociology, 34 (October 1975), pp. 365-379.

3. W. Richard Jacobs, "Factors Affecting Trade Union Organization and Development in Trinidad and Tobago" in W. Richard Jacobs et al., Seminar On Contemporary Issues No. 1: Labor and Industrial Relations in Trinidad and Tobago (Trinidad and Tobago: Faculty of Social Sciences, University of the West Indies, 1971), p. 17.

4. Ibid., pp. 17-19.

5. Selwyn D. Ryan, Race and Nationalism in Trinidad and Tobago: A Case Study of Decolonization in a Multiracial Society, (Toronto: University of Toronto Press, 1972) p. 61.

6. Ibid., pp. 74-76.

7. In addition to the works of Selwyn Ryan and Yogendra Malik referred to in Chapter 4, see also Krishna Bahadoorsingh, Trinidad Electoral Politics: The Persistence of the Race Factor (London: Institute of Race Relations, 1968).

8. Interview with author, Port-of-Spain, Trinidad, March 26, 1982.

9. Trinidad Guardian, November 28, 1961. Cited in Carl D. Parris, Capital or Labor? The Decision to Introduce the Industrial Stabilization Act in Trinidad and Tobago: Working Paper No. 2 (Jamaica: Institute of Social Economic Research, University of the West Indies, 1965), p. 14.

10. Yogendra K. Malik, East Indians in Trinidad: A Study in Minority Politics (London: Oxford University Press, 1971) p. 113.

11. Ibid., p. 119.

12. Ryan, Race and Nationalism, p. 258.

13. Malik, East Indians in Trinidad, pp. 119-120.

14. Charles W. Blowers, "The Industrial Development of Trinidad, 1952-1962," M.A. thesis, Department of Economics, University of Florida, 1964, pp. 121-123.

15. Industrial Development Corporation, Why Foreign Investment is Attracted to Trinidad and Tobago (Port-of-Spain, Trinidad: Yuille Printery Limited, 1962), pp. 13-16.

16. Ibid., p. 16.

17. Ibid., p. 9.

18. Henry Zin, Labor Relations and Industrial Conflict in Commonwealth Caribbean Countries (Port-of-Spain, Trinidad: Columbus Publishers Ltd., 1972).

19. OWTU, Oilfields Workers' Trade Union, July 1937-July 1977 (Trinidad and Tobago: Syncreators Ltd., 1977), p. 27.

20. Report of the Commission of Inquiry Into Subversive Activities in Trinidad and Tobago (Trinidad and Tobago: The Government Printery, 1965), p. 7.

21. Ibid., pp. 13-14.

22. Ibid., pp. 52-53.

23. Malik, East Indians in Trinidad, pp. 149-150.

24. Trevor Sudama, "Class, Race and the State in Trinidad and Tobago" (unpublished paper), p. 47.

25. R.D. Thomas, "The Next Step in Industrial Relations in Trinidad and Tobago," in W. Richard Jacobs et al., Seminar on Contemporary Issues No. 1: Labor and Industrial Relations in Trinidad and Tobago (Trinidad and Tobago: Faculty of Social Sciences, University of the West Indies, 1971), pp. 25-26.

26. Eric E. Williams, Inward Hunger: The Education of a Prime Minister (London: Andre Duetsch, 1969) p. 311. See also Eric E. Williams, Reflections on the Industrial Stabilization Act (Trinidad and Tobago: The Nation, 1965).

27. Trinidad Guardian, May 14, 1969, p. 1.

28. Trinidad Guardian, May 15, 1969, p. 1.

29. Interview with author, Port-of-Spain, Trinidad, March 30, 1982.

30. Trinidad Guardian, February 26, 1970, p. 1.

31. Trinidad Guardian, March 6, 1970, p. 15.

32. Trinidad Guardian, March 11, 1970, p. 11.

33. Trinidad Guardian, March 24, 1970, p. 6.

34. Trinidad Guardian, April 15, 1970, p. 8.

35. Trinidad Guardian, April 22, 1970, p. 1.

36. Trinidad Guardian, May 3, 1970, p.1. For a chronological summary of the Black Power demonstrations, see Ivar Oxaal, Race and Revolutionary Consciousness: A Documentary Interpretation of the 1970 Black Power Revolt in Trinidad (Cambridge, Mass.: Schenkman Publishing Company, 1971).

37. David G. Nichols, "East Indians and Black Power in Trinidad," Race 12 (April 1971), pp. 448-449.

38. Trinidad Guardian, August 1, 1970, p. 1.

39. Trinidad Guardian, October 17, 1969, p. 1.

40. OWTU, Oilfields Workers' Trade Union, pp. 37-38.

41. Ibid., p. 38.

42. Trade union leaders who were interviewed were especially bitter at the curtailment of their right to strike. They argued that the relocation of the industrial dispute into the industrial court puts them at a disadvantage relative to the companies because the latter can afford to retain better legal services.

43. Third Session Third Parliament Trinidad and Tobago, 21 Elizabeth II, Act No. 23 of 1972, The Industrial Relations Act.

44. Trinidad Guardian, April 3, 1975, p. 1. See also OWTU, Oilfields Workers' Trade Union, p. 39.

45. OWTU, Oilfields Workers' Trade Union, pp. 39-40.

46. Interview with author, Port-of-Spain, Trinidad, February 26, 1982.

47. OWTU, Oilfields Workers' Trade Union, p. 40.

48. Ibid.

49. Trinidad Guardian, March 11, 1975, p. 1. For a detailed account of the ULF march and interviews with some of its leaders, see Owen Baptiste, ed., Crisis (Trinidad: Inprint Caribbean Ltd., 1976).

50. Trinidad Guardian, March 31, 1975, p. 1.

51. Trinidad Guardian, August 15, 1970, p. 17.

52. Interview with author, Port-of-Spain, Trinidad, February 26, 1982.

53. Ibid.

54. Selwyn Ryan, "The Disunited Labour Front" (unpublished paper), 1978, p. 6.

55. Interview with author, Port-of-Spain, Trinidad, March 26, 1982.

56. Ibid.

6 MULTINATIONALS, THE STATE, AND THE MANAGEMENT OF ECONOMIC NATIONALISM

This chapter examines the relations between the PNM government[1] and the foreign companies in the oil and sugar industries, and the intersection between these relations and the domestic politics of the country. The principal argument is that national ownership of foreign companies was not dictated by a comprehensive plan or ideology, but occurred in piecemeal fashion in response to particular domestic pressures, and against foreign companies that were failing in their Trinidad operations or were indifferent to remaining in the country. In no case was the acquisition motivated by the prospect of financial gain. Rather, the acquisition of foreign-owned companies by the government was intended to save jobs, to appease nationalists, and to head off the drive for further nationalization of the more successful oil companies. In this latter goal, the success of the government was aided by the fact that the numerous state-run enterprises had acquired a reputation for inefficiency and had become a drain on the public treasury. Poor performance by state-acquired enterprises, particularly the sugar industry because of its size and the public knowledge that it is heavily subsidized, created a popular impression that nationalization does not work.

The settlement terms offered to the companies selected or put up for government purchase were generous enough to reassure other foreign investors already in the country that they did not have to fear for their operations in Trinidad. They also represented an extraordinary measure on the part of the government to preserve the image of the country as friendly to foreign investment.

THE PERIOD OF INNOCENCE (1956-1969)

Prior to Trinidad's independence in 1962, the oil industry was hardly affected by indigenous views of how the industry should evolve. The most vocal indigenous group on the question of oil was the oil union, the OWTU, and its demands were mainly for wages and a cessation of retrenchment of workers from the industry. Through political parties of its own creation, the union had called for the nationalization of the industry, but with little support either within or outside of the industry, this demand receded from prominence.

The period 1956 to 1962 was the PNM's first term in office. The PNM had little experience in administration, in general, and very little expertise in the oil business. As a result, the ruling party did not institute any new policies that would affect the operations of the oil companies in Trinidad. The companies were usually incorporated overseas. Changes in ownership took place abroad and were reflected in Trinidad by changes in company names and changes in management. For example, in 1956, the Trinidad Petroleum Development company was acquired by British Petroleum and became British Petroleum Trinidad Ltd. Also, the Trinidad Leaseholds Limited was bought over by Texaco in 1956 and became Texaco Trinidad Inc. The government of Trinidad simply watched from the sidelines. It was only the oil union that called upon the government to use these opportunities to acquire greater national control over the industry.

Until 1964, the oil industry, despite its preeminent position in the country's economy, was administered by a subdivision of the Ministry of Agriculture, called the Petroleum Department. This typified the lack of national emphasis on monitoring the country's key resource. Of course, it was a continuation of colonial policy, but it also reflected a lack of knowledge on the part of the new PNM government about the oil industry, both domestically and internationally. The only indigenous experience with the industry resided with the oil union, which advocated an approach to the industry that differed radically from the one contemplated by the government.

During its early years in power, the PNM government played the role of arbiter between the oil companies and the oil union, which was resorting to strike action to get wage increases and to stop the retrenchment of workers by the companies. The union claimed that between 1959 and 1961, more than 2000 workers had been laid off their jobs. The justification which the companies, particularly British Petroleum and Shell, put forward was that land production was falling and it would not be profitable to open up new wells. The companies also claimed that the oil industry internationally was in recession. In early 1963, British Petroleum announced its plans to lay off about 350 of its workers. In an attempt to stop the retrenchment, the oil union under George Weekes served strike notice to the company. On February 17, the workers at British Petroleum went on a strike that lasted 57 days.[2]

The apparent state of turmoil in the oil industry forced the government to initiate a two-pronged approach to the industry. Fearful that the country's oil reserves might indeed be rapidly dwindling, and lacking any independent means of confirming this, the government announced in April 1963 that it was setting up a commission of inquiry to look into the oil industry. The government also announced that a commission of inquiry would be set up to investigate subversive activities within the trade union movement (see Chapter 5). This latter inquiry seemed to have grown out of the government's fear of the increasing militancy of the oil union and, from the proceedings of this inquiry, it was clear that the inquiry was being used as a means of isolating the oil union within the trade union movement and of discrediting it in the eyes of the public.

The commission of inquiry into the oil industry was headed by Baghair Mustofi, an Iranian oil expert. The Mustofi Commission, as it is commonly called, held hearings intermittently between August 6, 1963 and June 30, 1964. The report outlined what the commission considered to be basic facts about the oil industry in Trinidad. Among these were the following:

1. There were serious limitations on the discovery of further oil reserves on land. Offshore exploration was recommended as the way to open up new reserves.
2. Because of the comparatively small volume of production and reserves in Trinidad, the world would not suffer any hardship if Trinidadian production were disrupted.
3. The reserve-to-production ratio of about 10:1 was so precarious that a very high flow of investment was required to keep production at its current level.
4. Because of the small productive potentials of wells, Trinidad was a comparatively high-cost producer, but the Trinidadian oil industry had remained competitive because of the low cost of its refining operations.[3]

The commission recommended that since there seemed to be little hope of a major expansion of crude-oil production, Trinidad should try to lead the world in efficient and low-cost refining operations. This it could do by cutting labor costs. Automation should be encouraged, and the workforce should be reduced to the lowest possible levels. Moreover, the government should try to ensure a general business climate favorable to investment. The commission also made recommendations for an overhaul of the administrative and legal framework governing the oil industry and for fiscal measures aimed at improving the country's revenue-collecting system as it affected oil.[4] These recommendations were incorporated into the Petroleum Act of 1969.

The commission's recommendations with regard to workforce requirements and labor costs for the refining operations, if implemented, meant a clampdown on the oil union since the union was not likely to accept those conditions. In addition, the government did not have the necessary capital for offshore exploration to increase its reserves. This meant that the source of capital would be foreign. To attract foreign investment it was necessary, as the commission again recommended, to create an attractive investment climate. An attractive investment climate was a prerequisite for the success of the government's general industrialization plan. The commission's recommendation, therefore, underscored the urgency for the government to address the issue. However, given the labor unrest that plagued the oil industry and the country in general, labor controls seemed inevitable. And the Industrial Stabilization Act of 1965 was the first move by the government in that direction (see Chapter 5).

The Mustofi Commission Report underscored the marginality of Trinidadian crude oil production. It confirmed the fears of government officials that the country's oil reserves were dwindling. It also had an adverse long-term effect on the development of local expertise to run the industry. As people learned that the future of the oil industry in Trinidad was bleak, very few were prepared to pattern their careers to fit higher technical positions within the industry. This trend was kept alive by the generally bleak picture that the local press has painted of the industry. Those who opted for a higher education in some aspect of the petroleum industry had to be educated overseas, and problems developed in inducing them to return to Trinidad.

The Mustofi Commission Report strengthened the bargaining position of the oil companies vis-à-vis the government. Given the state of the industry, the oil companies were simply interested in maintaining their concession terms intact. Of course, the government was in too weak a position to make demands on the companies. However, to ensure the preservation of the status quo, the companies played on the government's insecurity. In 1965, Texaco's chairman of the board made a speech on a visit to Trinidad that was carried in the local newspapers. He said: "We have carefully planned our producing capabilities and refining capacity over the world to put us in a flexible position. . . . If, for example, there is reduced production, for whatever reason, in one area we can immediately offset this by increases elsewhere."[5] In addition, officials from the oil companies periodically complained of the comparatively high cost of oil production in Trinidad or expressed their frustration at not being able to find additional oil. In fact, Shell and British Petroleum reduced their drilling activities significantly.

The gloomy prospects for the Trinidadian oil industry increased the government's sense of urgency about the need to diversify the economy. The government called a conference of the oil and sugar companies to solicit their active collaboration in its industrialization effort. The government proposed:

1. that the companies try to curtail the retrenchment of workers because it was aggravating an already serious unemployment problem;
2. that the companies assist in settling people on the land by making available unused land and doing some of the preparatory work such as clearing the land and building access roads;
3. that the companies assist in the setting up of industries that could utilize some of the byproducts of the oil and sugar industries, and also in developing markets for the products.

These proposals were rebuffed by the companies. The comments of the British Petroleum delegate typified the comments made by the delegates from Texaco, Shell and the sugar company, Caroni Ltd. He said,

We believe that we know our business, and it is with some diffidence that we enter into a discussion other than winning, refining and marketing of oil. . . . We cannot forget our responsibilities to our shareholders not to embark upon enterprises which we are not competent to operate.[6]

Although the government was unhappy about the outcome of this conference and about the unwillingness of the companies to cooperate, it did nothing. It issued no threats. It simply accepted the results, communicating by its inaction an unwillingness to offend foreign investors. This was the bargaining reputation that the government was developing, and the foreign companies would exploit it.

ACQUISITION OF BRITISH PETROLEUM

In January 1967, Shell announced that about 400 of its employees were to be laid off in a phased retrenchment. The company justified the need for this action by citing the bleak circumstances that it faced. Shell pointed out that land production was dwindling and secondary recovery methods had failed to increase land production. Further, the company argued that since there were no more suitable drilling locations on land, further drilling would cease. Finally, Shell claimed that falling prices and marketing difficulties had eroded the company's financial position, and there was a need for some cost-cutting action to shore up its position.[7]

Soon after Shell's announcement, British Petroleum (BP) called in the oil union officials to discuss its proposals for reducing its own workforce. British Petroleum planned to reduce its workforce by 75 percent within a short period of time. British Petroleum put forward the same reasons as Shell, claiming, however, that its situation with respect to production and drilling was worse than that of Shell. Further, British Petroleum offered its assets in Trinidad for sale.[8]

The PNM government knew that British Petroleum had tremendous reserves in Alaska and that the company had apparently been contemplating increasing its activities there. It needed money and was therefore cutting off less productive activities elsewhere to save costs. Its activities in Trinidad, which had a high labor content, fell into this category. The signs that British Petroleum was leaving had been evident for some time: Its exploration activities had ceased and a widespread redundancy program had been in progress.

The government attempted to get Shell and Texaco to buy over the BP assets, but both turned down the offer. The oil union tried to persuade the government to set up a national oil company and purchase the assets of British Petroleum. The OWTU, showing some sensitivity to the policy of the government to eschew nationalization of foreign enterprise, made a persuasive argument for government acquisition. The OWTU argued that it was not advocating nationalization in the sense of confiscation of private property. Rather, an enterprise was available for sale and there seemed to be no private buyers. The consequences of inaction would be mass unemployment in an economy already plagued by high unemployment rates, loss of revenue to the government, and the adverse multiplier effects on the rest of the economy. Under these circumstances, the oil union encouraged the government to pay reasonable compensation to BP and acquire the assets.[9]

However, the Williams government panicked. It felt that the country had neither the technical and managerial skills to run the BP operations nor the marketing expertise to dispose of the crude petroleum. When both Texaco and Shell declined its offer to buy over the BP assets, the government was in a quandary. It was aware of the political, economic, and social consequences that would accompany a collapse of this segment of the oil industry. It was certain that no major company would get involved, so it began to look for a small company. Yet the prospect of inviting in a new foreign investor to completely take over the BP assets was troublesome. The reason for this was that the government had been voicing disillusionment with its policy of "industrialization by invitation" and had been advocating a greater role for the state in the economy. It could not entirely pass up this opportunity to make good on its promise. On the other hand, it did not have the expertise to run an oil company. The government eventually decided to acquire the BP assets in 1969 in a joint venture with a new foreign investor.

Two good indications of the state of confusion that existed within the government as it confronted the problem posed by the intended withdrawal of British Petroleum were the compensation paid to BP for its property and the choice of the joint-venture partner. The compensation that British Petroleum demanded for its properties was excessive. The book value of BP's properties was $14.3 million, but BP demanded more than double this amount.[10] In addition, it was demanding compensation for oil in the ground in the soon-to-be-abandoned oil fields. BP's bargaining position was very weak. BP had claimed that further operation in Trinidad would not be profitable. This claim devalued the worth of its property to any prospective buyer contemplating continuing the same business. The value of the property was further diminished by the fact that none of the major companies operating in Trinidad wanted to buy BP's property. Yet the Williams government made a very generous settlement with BP. It agreed to pay BP $22 million in cash and oil, and within a year, BP was completely paid off.[11] The justification for this generous settlement was that the government did not want to be accused of "nationalizing" foreign investors and scaring away incoming foreign capital; neither did it want any future interference with the state company from a dissatisfied BP.

The government chose as its joint-venture partner a relatively unknown American oil company called Tesoro Petroleum Company, whose operations were based in Texas. Tesoro had been discovered by the Minister of Petroleum and Mines, John O'Hallaran, on one of his trips to the United States. Tesoro's assets in 1969 amounted to $69 million, as compared to Texaco's US$8.6 billion. Tesoro's operations produced about 3250 barrels of oil per day and had a refinery throughput of 13,000 barrels per day. The company had no foothold outside of the United States.[12] However, within government circles, Tesoro was touted as having the necessary expertise in secondary recovery to arrest the declining yield of land fields. Tesoro's presumed ability to borrow from U.S. capital markets was also a major attraction to the Trinidadian government.

The proposal was that the Trinidadian government would own 50.1 percent of the new company, while Tesoro would own the remaining 49.9 percent. However, this split in the ownership was not reflected in the respective contributions for the British Petroleum properties that were bought for $22 million. Tesoro brought into Trinidad only $50,000 and with an additional $50,000 put up by the Trinidadian government, the Trinidad Tesoro Oil Company was launched.

Tesoro was instrumental in the new company's borrowing $25 million from several sources. Part of this was used to pay for the BP assets. Of the total sum borrowed, Tesoro acted as the guarantor for $7.5 million, while the government guaranteed the rest. However, as Farrell points out, given the fact that Tesoro was in a partnership with the government of Trinidad, which was not in any danger of bankruptcy, Tesoro carried no risks at all.[13] Further, despite Tesoro's small contribution to the new company, it demanded, and was granted, a management contract that gave it control over the financial, technological, and marketing operations of the company. The chairman of the company had to be approved by Tesoro and major decisions of the board of directors required a two-thirds majority of the board. By virtue of its appointment of four of the nine members of the board, Tesoro had a veto over these decisions. As Farrell puts it, "This was clearly a case of David buying Goliath."[14]

The first point that should be made about the acquisition of the BP assets by the Trinidadian government in the joint venture with Tesoro is that the action was not initiated by the government in fulfillment of any policy or development plan. Rather, it was a frantic response to a crisis situation posed by BP's declaration that it wanted to pull out of Trinidad because of the lack of profitability of its undertaking there. Even before the Mustofi Commission Report, it was known that the land reserves were dwindling. The Mustofi Report merely confirmed this. BP's withdrawal decision, based on the depletion of the land fields, shook the confidence of the government and gave it a glimpse of what lay in store if new reserves were not found. Henceforth, the threat of withdrawal by an oil company would be a potent threat indeed. In the absence of governmental intervention, the immediate consequences of a BP withdrawal would have been the retrenchment of workers into an economy already plagued by a high unemployment rate, and loss of revenue to the government. The action taken by the government was a last resort action. It was more in the nature of a rescue operation: to save jobs and to prevent the social disruption that would ensue from mass retrenchment. The final settlement with BP showed the government's anxiety to preserve the image of the country as an attractive environment for foreign investment, or at least one that did not pose a threat to foreign enterprise.

Senior officials at the Ministry of Energy who were interviewed by the author in 1982 appeared embarrassed by the handling of the BP purchase and particularly by the Tesoro deal. The terms with which the government secured the partnership of Tesoro were evidence of the inexperience of the government in dealing with MNCs and a lack of knowledge of the oil business even after 13 years in office. The circumstances surrounding BP's departure strengthened Tesoro's position. Since the government felt that the expertise to run BP's operations was not available locally and since Tesoro possessed the expertise in secondary recovery methods and promised to make the enterprise a profitable one, the government acceded to its demand for control over the financial, technological, and marketing operations of the new company.

THE PETROLEUM ACT OF 1969

The first significant piece of oil legislation initiated by the PNM came after 13 years in office. This was Act No. 46 of 1969 and its accompanying Petroleum Regulations which came out in early 1970. The Act was largely the work of Dr. Fuad Rouhani, the first OPEC secretary-general, who had been invited to Trinidad to work on the legislation. The Act was a codification of the recommendations of the Mustofi Report. It was an attempt to bring licensing arrangements and fiscal obligations of the oil companies operating in Trinidad more in line with the prevailing practice in the major oil-producing countries. Licenses were to be granted on the basis of open competitive bidding. The Petroleum Regulations established a stricter framework under which exploration activities would be carried out in Trinidad.

The Petroleum Act of 1969 made a few changes in the fiscal obligations imposed on prospective investors. Under the old laws, companies operating in Trinidad were required to pay royalty charges on their crude oil production, an oil impost to defray the administrative costs to the government of running the Ministry of Petroleum and Mines, licensing fees for the privilege of operating in Trinidad, and corporation taxes amounting to 42.5 percent of taxable income.[15] The new law added to these a surface rent associated with the area licensed to the companies. This was a very modest increase in the fiscal obligations of the companies. However, the law reduced the submarine depletion allowance from 20 percent to 10 percent of the gross value of production for companies holding submarine oil mining licenses granted prior to 1961. The Petroleum Regulations required a company to construct a refinery with a throughput capacity of 50 percent of the aggregate average daily production in cases where the aggregate average daily production exceeded 100,000 barrels per day. Construction of a refinery was also required if the company's average exceeded 50,000 barrels per day and the aggregate proven reserves were sufficient to support continuation of aggregate average daily production of 100,000 barrels per day for a future continuous period of seven and one-half years.[16]

The government's decision to lower the submarine well allowance was no doubt motivated by the expectation of increased drilling activity in submarine areas after the well-publicized oil discovery by Amoco off the east coast of Trinidad in 1968. Nevertheless, the Petroleum Act of 1969 and the government's acquisition of the British Petroleum assets put the government in a better position to monitor developments in the oil industry at home and abroad.

THE CLAMOR FOR REDUCED FOREIGN ECONOMIC CONTROL

By the late 1960s, the government had decided that its industrialization plan was not working. The economy was still heavily dependent on oil
and sugar, and the manufacturing sector was underdeveloped and confined to
the production of such commodities as soap, detergents, and some assembly-
type industries. In 1968, almost mid-way in its third term of office, the
government published the draft of its Third Five-Year Plan which was
approved the following year. The period covered by the plan was 1969 to
1973. The main tasks that the plan addressed were the diversification of the
country's structure of production, the achievement of full employment, and
the necessity to set the economy on a more self-reliant footing.[17]

The government registered its disenchantment with the contribution
of foreign companies to the country's development goals and outlined a new
role that the state should play in promoting its economic goals. The state
was to play a greater role in controlling the "commanding heights" of the
economy, which included the banks, the mass media, public utilities,
manufacturing industries, sugar, oil, and petrochemicals. The plan
recognized the low and stagnant level of local entrepreneurship and hoped to
upgrade local management and supervisory skills by carving out a greater
role for government in running the industries traditionally reserved for
foreign enterprise, namely oil and sugar.[18] No timetable was spelled out for
the plan.

However, pressure on the government to move ahead with these
objectives came from the Black Power demonstrations of February and
March of 1970 (see Chapter 5). The Black Power revolution, as it is
commonly referred to in Trinidad, was a revolt of urban blacks, primarily
youths, against the PNM government. The blacks felt that the PNM had
failed to fulfill the promises it had made with regard to the economic uplift of
blacks in Trinidad. The Black Power militants cited, as evidence of the
PNM's betrayal, the control that foreign companies continued to exercise
over the economy, as well as the predominant position of the local white
population in such areas as banking and commerce. The Black Power
revolution was supported by several trade unions, including the OWTU, and
by an army revolt which was eventually subdued. The Black Power militants
marched into the sugar belt to enlist the support of Indian sugar workers.
This effort did not succeed since the Indians felt threatened by the Black
Power movement.

The PNM government tried to address some of the grievances of the
Black Power demonstrators. The government announced that it would
nationalize foreign-owned banks and insurance companies. Second, the
government bought over 51 percent of the holdings in the sugar industry as a
first step toward improving conditions in the industry. Third, the PNM
recognized the urgency of incorporating the dissident component of its
following into the economic life of the country. This it did by encouraging
the development of small businesses by blacks, and by providing employment
through an expanded "special works" program (see Chapter 2). The
government also imposed a 5 percent unemployment levy on individuals and
companies whose taxable income exceeded $10,000. The effect of this on the

oil and sugar companies was an increase in the corporation tax from 42.5 percent to 47.5 percent. These companies accepted the increase in tax without protest, because the alternative was much more frightening. With a mob at its heels, the government's bargaining power vis-à-vis the foreign companies had increased.

At this point, it would be very instructive to examine why the sugar industry was chosen at this juncture for equity participation by the state. Given the strong call for local control from dissident elements within the ranks of the PNM and the government's public statements of sympathy, something needed to be done. The most conspicuous areas of foreign control were the oil and sugar industries. Only the year before, the government had panicked when confronted with the possibility of having to run British Petroleum by itself. It was not now prepared to confront another oil company with its limited experience. On the other hand, it needed to placate those elements advocating economic nationalism. The sugar industry seemed the least harmful to confront, and some degree of involvement there promised enormous political payoffs.

The sugar industry, organized on the basis of plantations, carried with it the stigma of slavery and indentureship. Prime Minister Eric Williams had written extensively on slavery and on sugar[19] and had promised before he was voted into office to expunge the sugar industry of the ill effects of the plantation system. The only way he could do this was by acquiring some degree of control. However, 14 years had elapsed and still the government had done nothing to change fundamentally the structure and mode of operations of the sugar industry. In the meantime, radical groups opposed to the government were attempting to make common cause with the sugar workers, and since sugar workers determined the elections in 12 electoral constituencies, success by the radicals would give them a sizable foothold in the political arena. Further, since the radical elements associated with the OWTU and NJAC were predominantly black, courtship of the Indians in the sugar belt carried great political significance.

The venture posed a great risk to the PNM's aspirations for longevity in office. The claim of bridging the racial division between the Indians and the blacks could greatly undermine the basis of electoral support for Williams and the PNM. Instead of race, class would become the basis of mobilizing electoral support. If, therefore, the PNM wanted to remain unchallenged in government, it was in its interest to keep the two races apart, or at least to ensure that Indian sugar workers would not fall under the leadership of radical blacks. One way of doing this was to improve conditions in the sugar industry. This would remove some of the long-felt grievances of the sugar workers and would make them less susceptible to the radical positions taken by NJAC and the OWTU. It would also shore up the position of conservative leadership of the sugar union, which, apart from being pro-business, felt that the Black Power movement was anti-Indian.

The sugar industry seemed a safe enterprise for state involvement for another important reason. Despite the stated intention of the government to become more actively involved in the economy, private foreign investment was still welcome. The government, through the Industrial Stabilization Act, had attempted to create a more stable investment climate by setting up the framework for the speedy resolution of industrial disputes. However, there were indications that the major sugar company, Caroni Ltd., was preparing to leave Trinidad. Sugar production in Trinidad reached its peak in 1965 and thereafter began a steep decline. In 1966 and 1967, Caroni Ltd. reported a loss.[20] Further, as Britain readied to enter the European Common Market, the future of Caribbean sugar, which entered Britain on a preferential quota basis, seemed uncertain. In Trinidad, labor costs were increasing rapidly, particularly with the oil industry setting a high pace in wage rates. In April 1970, the Industrial Court settled a wage dispute between the sugar union and Caroni Ltd. in favor of the union.[21] The workers were granted a generous wage increase despite Caroni's pleading its inability to pay. Caroni then offered its sugar cane lands for sale to the government. There were reports that Caroni was running down its factories. In short, the writing was on the wall that Caroni Ltd. was planning to leave Trinidad. Since the sugar industry was the largest employer of labor, outside of the government, the impact on unemployment and the resulting social disruptions were easy to imagine.

The political payoffs for government acquisition of majority interest in Caroni were enormous. In the first place, the company welcomed it. The cost to the government for 51 percent of the ordinary shares was $5 million and the company seemed satisfied with the settlement. Because the government had acquired these shares in a rescue operation, the country's image of being friendly to foreign companies would be preserved. On the other hand, the government appeared as the benefactor of the sugar workers by ensuring the security of their jobs and appearing to be following through on its promise to improve conditions in the sugar industry. Further, in partial appeasement of those who stridently advocated greater national control of the economy, the government could claim credit for acquiring majority control in the oldest multinational corporation operating in the country, thereby relieving some of the pressure for the government to move against the much more profitable oil industry. Further acquisitions were not financially possible: The funds in the government's coffers were running down. By September 1973, the government was confronted with a grave financial crisis. The Trinidadian Treasury had just enough money for the payment of salaries to civil servants for a period of three months.[22] However, this situation changed dramatically with the OPEC price increases.

NJAC, the spearhead of the Black Power movement, was not satisfied with the actions taken by the PNM government. It accused the government of engaging in tokenism, and it scoffed at the joint-venture arrangements into which the government had entered. In a publication entitled Slavery to Slavery, the NJAC made the following complaint:

> The Government under pressure from the people is engaging in some tokenism. They took a piece of Tate & Lyle [Caroni Ltd.] on hire purchase, they bought a token bank and a token share of oil, they say. Nothing meaningful. And we can't even claim these things for Black People. . . .

When the Government invests in oil and sugar they are going in to joint ventures with foreigners; they are wasting our money to finance the pillars of a system which is anti-black. These companies operate as parts of large multi-national corporations. They base decisions on what is in the best interest of a whole international complex. So all this foolishness about setting up boards with local chairmen is game-playing, expensive game-playing, because we know none of the important decisions are made here anyway. What we want is ownership and control, not ownership in name. We are too much in need to be overpaying these people for company shares as political gimmicks (emphasis added).[23]

Nevertheless, the NJAC and its supporters had succeeded in drawing national attention to the dominant role of foreign enterprise in the Trinidadian economy.

THE NATIONALIZATION OF SHELL

In 1974, the Trinidadian government nationalized the holdings of Shell Trinidad Ltd. The OPEC price regime was in effect and many producer countries began to exercise increasing control over their oil industries. Indeed, international market conditions for petroleum and the precedent provided by several developing countries in dealing with their oil industries created a climate that might be described as propitious for the nationalization of such an industry. The Trinidadian government had enunciated a policy of increasing its control over oil and sugar in 1968. This commitment was reaffirmed in the midst of the Black Power demonstrations. The Trinidadian government could not ignore the opportunities now available without incurring severe political costs. This was recognized by the delegates at the fifteenth annual convention of the PNM in December 1973. The convention recommended that the government seek a larger share in the nation's oil business. In order to prepare the ground for governmental action, the convention passed the following resolution:

Be it resolved that this Convention recommends to Government that a special study be urgently undertaken with the purpose of ascertaining the feasibility of Government acquiring majority shareholdings in the producing fields of Shell Limited and Texaco Trinidad, Inc.[24]

The wording of the resolution gave the government a great amount of flexibility. It was clear that the party was not pressing the government to nationalize any of the companies but simply to get involved with them on a joint-venture basis. With this party mandate, the government approached Shell.

In 1974, Shell was the smallest of the four major producing companies in Trinidad (Amoco, Texaco and Trinidad Tesoro were the others: see Tables 3.2 and 3.3). In 1974, Shell accounted for about 13 percent of Trinidad's crude oil production. Only about one-quarter of Shell's production came from its own land fields, while the rest came from Shell's participation in the Trinidad Northern Areas consortium. Since the late 1960s it seemed as though Shell had been planning to leave Trinidad. Shell had not opened a new oil field since 1963. It had curtailed drilling activity and had begun to lay off workers. It seemed as though the company was going to tap flowing oil, without investing any additional sums, and then depart. Shell, like BP before it, was interested in withdrawing from its least productive areas and expanding in more lucrative areas such as the North Sea and the U.S. offshore. The willingness of Shell to leave, especially in light of production trends in Trinidad, made it a safe target for nationalization and promised to yield the same political payoffs as had the government's equity participation in the sugar company Caroni Ltd.

There was, however, an additional dimension to the Shell problem. Shell owned and operated a refinery at Point Fortin, whose rated capacity was 100,000 barrels per day. The Point Fortin refinery was old and antiquated. The refinery produced fuel oil for export to the United States, through Shell outlets, but it also served to make feedstock for further processing at the Shell refinery in Curacao. Shell was interested in holding onto its Point Fortin refinery. There was a natural market for the products of the refinery in the Caribbean Common Market countries. Thus, although Shell would have terminated its production operations, it wanted to maintain a presence in Trinidad. This consideration was probably uppermost in the minds of top Shell officials when the company made an offer to the government for the latter to buy into the company.

During the ensuing negotiations between the government and Shell, the government came under pressure from two sources to buy over the entire company. The first came from Tesoro, which urged the government to nationalize Shell and turn the company over to Trinidad Tesoro. In return, the government's share in the resulting merger would be increased to 60 percent of the equity. On the other hand, there was a strong feeling within government circles that the government should own a refinery. The principal argument was that the government could use the Point Fortin refinery to establish forward linkages with the economy. Byproducts of the refining process could be used as feedstocks for a petrochemical industry. Because of the windfall that arose from the OPEC price increases, the government had the money to make the purchase alone. In addition, the Ministry of Petroleum and Mines had much greater experience and confidence with the oil industry than in 1969 when it was confronted with the prospect of taking over the British Petroleum assets in Trinidad. In the end, the government declined the Tesoro offer and Shell was nationalized by the government. Shell's holdings, including the Point Fortin refinery, were vested in the newly created state company, Trinidad and Tobago Oil Company (TRINTOC). The payment to Shell was a very generous $44 million, with part payable in cash, and part in oil. Within a year the company was completely paid off. As a senior executive of TRINTOC and a former employee of Shell put it, it was important to arrive at a settlement wherein the government would be guaranteed non-interference by Shell in the future operations of TRINTOC and would be able to maintain its reputation as friendly to foreign investment.[25]

Although there were complaints about the price paid for Shell's assets, the acquisition was generally well received in Trinidad. However, the nationalization of Shell whetted the radicalism of groups such as the OWTU. Shortly after Shell was taken over, the OWTU began its "Texaco must go" campaign.

THE 1974 PETROLEUM TAXES ACT

Trinidad is not a member of OPEC. Its application for membership was turned down on the ground that it was a net importer of petroleum. Trinidad, therefore, had no influence over the petroleum price increases levied by the OPEC countries. In fact, because Trinidad is a marginal producer of petroleum, it has never influenced the world price of this commodity. After 1973, however, the new role assumed by the major producing countries and reflected in vastly improved market conditions for oil, strengthened the bargaining position of the Trinidadian government relative to the foreign oil companies operating in the country. The quadrupling of petroleum prices after 1973 provided the Trinidadian government with an opportunity to renegotiate its position with the oil companies. It was safe to do this since it would merely be following an international precedent. It would be asking of the oil companies no more for its oil than these companies were paying elsewhere.

The readjustment in the government's bargaining position with the oil companies was reflected in the Petroleum Taxes Act passed in June 1974. The Act spelled out new procedures for the taxation of the petroleum companies. For the purpose of taxation, the Act classified all petroleum operations into three separate businesses, even though the same corporate entity may carry on more than one of these. The categories were exploration and production operations, refining operations, and marketing operations. For any petroleum production business, a 47.5 percent tax was levied on taxable profits. This was increased to 50 percent in 1975. A 45 percent tax was levied on the marketing business. With regard to the refining operations, a throughput tax was imposed on every standard unit of crude oil passed through the refinery, regardless of the profit position of the company engaged in the refining business.[26]

The 1974 Petroleum Taxes Act was a major revision of petroleum taxation in Trinidad. Previously, the major tax levied against the operating companies was a corporation tax. The companies could, through a manipulation of transfer prices, make their overall profits from all areas of operation in Trinidad appear smaller than they really were. For example, until this time, much of the oil that Texaco refined at the Pointe-à-Pierre refinery was brought in, under a processing agreement, from its subsidiaries in other parts of the world. The processing fee per barrel of crude oil bore no relation to the value added by the refining process. The processing fee per barrel of crude oil was frequently just enough to cover the cost of refining it or even slightly below that cost, so that Texaco, in its refining operations, would show zero profit or a loss that could be deducted from the taxes it paid on its other operations.[27] The new law prevented the abuse of transfer prices and guaranteed the government a larger income from taxes levied against the oil companies.

An important aspect of the new law was the determination of the profits of the companies in the three separate areas of business. The key factor in this determination was the per barrel petroleum price used. The new law provided that profit calculations were to be based on tax reference prices determined by the government. In order to arrive at these tax reference prices, a reference crude oil from another country was first chosen, based on its similarity with the Trinidadian crude oil with respect to density, sulphur content, and so on. Two reference crudes were chosen: the Nigerian bonny light for the higher quality crude produced from offshore wells and the Venezuelan tiajuana for the oil produced from the land wells. The OPEC prices of the two crude oils were adjusted to reflect minor differences between the Trinidadian crudes and the reference crudes. The resulting prices were used as the tax reference prices in Trinidad. The method of using tax reference prices for the purpose of taxation provided the Trinidadian government with greater control over the oil industry because it could independently assess the increased revenues due to the price increases. In effect, the government now decided the price by which it would tax the oil companies. Of course, this new method of taxation was neither new nor radical. Trinidad was merely following current international practices, but within the domestic political context the propaganda value was enormous.

The Act was made retroactive to January 1, 1974. The enormous increases in government revenues and the general prosperity of the country were all credited to the government. There was no opposition in this parliament since the government had won all seats in parliament in the 1971 election owing to a boycott of the election by opposition parties. Further, the apparent ability of the government to dictate prices to the oil companies and the increased control over the industry that this conferred on the government, compounded with the state's participation with Trinidad Tesoro and ongoing nationalization discussions with Shell, lent credence to the government's claim that it was following through on its promise to control, inter alia, the oil industry. It also served to divert attention from the fact that the major companies, Amoco and Texaco, were still operating free of government control and continued to dominate the Trinidadian oil industry.

By the end of August 1974, the government had acquired the properties of Shell. The government kept up the momentum by passing in December 1974 the Petroleum (Amendment) Act of 1974, which amended the Petroleum Act of 1969 to allow the Minister of Petroleum and Mines to enter into production-sharing contracts with any company seeking to carry out exploration and production operations after November 1, 1974. Previously, an exploration and production license was granted to the company. Now the government reserved the right to share in the production of petroleum after a company's exploration had determined that commercial production was possible from a new discovery. Although this assertiveness was given a great deal of publicity, it should be pointed out that since the late 1960s, no major discovery has been made. The production-sharing contracts are a good insurance for the future, since they spell out in advance the degree of participation the government would get. However, none of the major producers of crude oil in Trinidad is operating under production-sharing contracts. Once again, this piece of legislation merely deflected any thrust for serious government action against Amoco and Texaco. However, unanticipated labor unrest in the oil and sugar industries put the government on the defensive again.

THE NATIONALIZATION OF CARONI LTD.

The central demand of the 1975 labor demonstrations (see Chapter 5) was for the nationalization of the foreign companies in the oil and sugar industries. The motto adopted was "Tate and Lyle and Texaco must go." The nationalization demand was the basis for the formation of the United Labor Front. Anxious to defuse the state of tension existing in the country, the PNM government moved expeditiously to nationalize the sugar company Caroni Ltd. The government was the majority shareholder, and it was aware that Tate and Lyle, the minority shareholder, would not be an unwilling seller. Thus the government was certain that nationalization of the sugar industry would not endanger the image of the country as a hospitable site for foreign investment.

On the other hand, nationalization of the sugar industry promised enormous political payoffs domestically. The sugar industry was not performing well and needed huge injections of capital which the government was in a position to provide largely because of the increased oil revenues. By subsidizing the sugar industry, the government would appear as the benefactor of the sugar workers and the government could expect greater cooperation from the sugar union. Also, since the continued subsidization of the sugar industry depended on the uninterrupted flow of revenues from the oil industry, it was possible for the government to wean the sugar union away from a position of rigid support for the nationalization of the oil industry. If this happened, the drive for the nationalization of the oil industry, as represented by the ULF, would be blunted. It would then be relatively easy for the government to isolate the oil union by claiming that the country's new prosperity was a verification of the correctness of the government's policy toward the oil industry. A simple cataloging of the government's role in TRINTOC, in Trinidad Tesoro, and in overhauling petroleum taxation to win for the country a lion's share of the profits from its petroleum, as well as the production-sharing contracts with new investors, would buttress the government's claim. In fact, by the end of 1977, this was precisely the situation that existed. The nationalization of the sugar industry satisfied a central demand of the sugar union. The union's leadership was thereafter under less pressure to go along with the radical demands of its partners and could more strongly assert its more moderate political positions. The ULF splintered and the nationalization drive lost its potency.

The PNM government was naturally pleased with this development. Its political fortunes seemed assured and it felt less impelled to confront the remaining foreign oil companies. However, there were clear signs of dissatisfaction among these companies.

MNC CLAMOR FOR A TAX REVISION

The U.S.-based oil companies were not happy with the system of petroleum taxation established by the 1974 Petroleum Taxes Act. In particular, they objected to the use of reference prices in the determination of their tax liabilities. The companies argued that they were not getting tax credits in the United States for taxes paid to the Trinidadian government because the Internal Revenue Service of the United States regarded the Trinidadian tax reference prices as arbitrary since they were not market-determined prices. The result was an erosion of the profit position of the companies. Further, the companies argued that the method of taxation was discriminatory since Trinidad Tesoro's tax liabilities were computed on the basis of realized prices.

Amoco and Texaco lobbied hard for a change in the tax system. To apply pressure on the government, the companies slowed down their exploration and drilling activities, and did not show much interest in continuing their operations in Trinidad.[28] In 1979, the government offered 11 blocks for exploration. Although 18 companies purchased the seismic data, only four companies submitted bids on three blocks. The state-owned company was the sole bidder on two of the blocks.[29] The lack of interest by the foreign companies alarmed the government to such an extent that it acceded to the companies' demand to amend the 1974 Petroleum Taxes Act.

In May 1981, the 1974 Petroleum Taxes Act was amended to introduce a new system of oil taxation. The prices used in calculating the companies' tax obligations were to be the actual market or realized prices instead of reference prices. A Supplemental Petroleum Tax was to be levied on the realized income of each company. The rate of this tax was 35 percent of gross income derived from land production and 60 percent of gross income derived from marine production. However, these computations were to be made after the deduction of a series of exceedingly generous capital and production allowances. The rate of the Petroleum Profits Tax set at 47.5 percent in 1974, and adjusted to 50 percent in 1975, was reduced to a corporation tax of 45 percent, the same as that for non-oil corporations. The much-vaunted refinery throughput tax was replaced by a general corporation tax. However, a Supplemental Refining Tax of $0.05 was imposed on each barrel of throughput for full refining, and $0.02 per barrel for light refining. The Supplemental Tax was deductible in computing the Petroleum Profits Tax.[30]

The new system of taxation was made retroactive to January 1, 1980. It was a clear capitulation to the oil companies. Its purpose was to induce the oil companies to remain in the country. However, while the oil companies preferred the new tax regime to the old, they were still not satisfied. They continued to lobby the government for a reduction in the

Supplemental Petroleum Tax. Further, the change in the tax regime proved inadequate to keep Texaco.

THE ACQUISITION OF TEXACO

Texaco traditionally enjoyed good relations with the PNM government. During the period 1962 to 1973, the relationship between the government and Texaco was especially cordial. Soon after Trinidad's independence, Texaco bought independence development bonds from the government at very low interest rates, a gesture that was greatly appreciated by the government. Further, Texaco chose Trinidad to be the base of its refining operations. In 1963, Texaco expanded its petrochemical operations in Trinidad when it installed a lube oil plant at Pointe-à-Pierre. During the 1960s, the government's financial position fluctuated precariously. To keep itself afloat, the government frequently approached the oil companies, particularly Texaco, for advance payments of taxes. Texaco frequently accommodated the government in those times of financial trouble. All of these contributed to a state of friendly relations between the government and Texaco.

However, a transition began to take place in the Trinidadian oil industry toward the end of the 1960s. In 1969, the government entered the oil-producing business when, in partnership with Tesoro, it bought the properties of British Petroleum. In 1974, the government acquired Shell, which it ran as a wholly government-owned company called TRINTOC. This greatly increased the confidence of the government, which began to speak of acquiring a greater share of the industry. The government seemed particularly keen on acquiring a controlling interest in the Texaco refinery at Pointe-à-Pierre. In such a position, the government hoped to widen the refinery operations to include the production of petrochemicals.

Texaco sought to preempt any significant government involvement in its major operations by inviting the government into a joint venture in petrochemicals. The proposed project involved the use of aromatic fibers from the refinery to make detergents. However, during the 1975 labor demonstrations in which the OWTU allied with the sugar union and called for the nationalization of Texaco, the company withdrew its proposals for a joint venture, cryptically pleading market reasons.

As has been pointed out before, the emergence of the ULF and the crowds that it drew in 1975 worried the government. The call for the nationalization of Texaco at a time when most oil-producing countries had intervened in their respective industries was one to which the government had to respond, especially in view of the fact that it was going to face a national election the next year. In January 1976, the government announced a team of negotiators, headed by Bernard Primus, chairman of the Industrial Development Corporation, to negotiate the acquisition of a controlling interest (51 percent) in Texaco's operations in Trinidad.

The government argued that no oil-producing country could be content to confine its activity in the industry to the collection of taxes and royalties, and that participation was the natural right of the country.[31]

Texaco seemed prepared to discuss government participation in the production sector but was adamant in its refusal to discuss participation in the refining operations. It was the feeling of some members of the government negotiating team that Texaco kept two separate sets of books on its refining operations--one that accurately reflected its operations, and one that it presented to the government for the purposes of taxation. Comparisons between the refining operations at the state-owned TRINTOC refinery with those of Texaco had given government officials reasons for concern, and it was felt that Texaco was determined to keep out the government so that the discrepancies would not be exposed.

During the negotiations, Texaco received support from the United States embassy in Trinidad. On June 6, 1976, the Trinidad Guardian carried, as its lead article, a letter from U.S. Ambassador Albert B. Fay to the government and to the heads of multinational corporations operating in Trinidad. The document, which was entitled "United States Government Policy Concerning Valuation of Expropriated Property," claimed to be reiterating and clarifying U.S. policy concerning the expropriation of property of its citizens by foreign governments.[32] The Trinidadian government was negotiating the purchase of 51 percent of Texaco. It had no plans to expropriate Texaco's property. However, by deliberately exaggerating the government's position, Ambassador Fay forced the government into a very defensive position. Eventually the negotiations were allowed to lapse. The government committee has never published a report of the negotiations. This was the first instance that a foreign company in Trinidad had stoutly refused to sell its properties, and the government backed down. The internal problems of the ULF during this period diverted domestic attention from the government's negotiations with Texaco, and the government was thereby relieved of significant pressure to maintain its original demand for equity participation, since the ULF had been the principal source of this pressure.

Toward the end of the 1970s, it became evident that Texaco was shifting its emphasis away from Trinidad. Its exploration effort was far less intensive than that of Trinidad Tesoro. The volume of crude oil passed through its refinery began to decline. In fact, Texaco closed down a sizable proportion of its refinery capacity. The government also noticed that Texaco was not as aggressive as some of the other companies, such as Amoco, in bidding for new acreages for exploration. In 1978, the OWTU accused Texaco of not acting in the "national interest" of Trinidad. The union charged that Texaco was running down its refinery; that is, it was not carrying out required equipment repair and machinery replacement. Further, the union pointed out, Texaco did not apply the same environmental standards in Trinidad as it did in the United States. The union also charged that Texaco was putting its shipping facilities at the disposal of South Africa. Given the fact that Trinidad has a large black population, and resentment of the South African regime runs deep, the government felt pressured to investigate Texaco's connection with South Africa. In 1979, the government instituted a commission of inquiry into Texaco's operations.

Although the commission conducted hearings, no final report was ever rendered. Texaco never appeared before the commission. In any case, other considerations superseded the government's concern about Texaco's South African connections. By 1982, it was not clear to the government whether Texaco would remain in Trinidad. Not only was Texaco running down the refinery, but it had also considerably reduced the volume of crude oil imported for refining in Trinidad, and it was not drilling new wells.

The uncertainty about Texaco's intentions prompted the government to undertake another investigation. In July 1982, Prime Minister George Chambers announced the appointment of a team of ministers to look into the future role of Texaco in Trinidad.[33] Pursuant to its charge, the team began holding discussions with Texaco. At the same time, the oil union was pressuring Texaco to state clearly whether it intended to continue operating in Trinidad and under what conditions it would do so.[34]

In December 1982, Texaco's general manager Lloyd Austin made it known that he did not see the company operating in Trinidad beyond the end of January 1983. He also indicated that the company might have to shut down the refinery.[35] In fact, at the end of 1982, Texaco ceased the importation of crude oil for refining at its Pointe-à-Pierre refinery. In order to keep the refinery running at a minimum level and thereby avert a domestic gasoline shortage, the government worked out an interim agreement with Texaco, by which the government-owned oil company TRINTOC would supply the refinery with 37,000 barrels of crude oil per day, and Texaco would supply an additional 28,000 barrels of crude oil per day. The agreement was intended to last until March 1983. However, since Texaco refused to import any crude oil, the arrangement between TRINTOC and Texaco continued until the end of the year.[36] As an inducement to Texaco to remain in Trinidad, the government also decided to reduce the rate of the Supplemental Petroleum Tax for land production from 35 percent to 15 percent.[37] However, at the end of 1983, Texaco offered to sell the Pointe-à-Pierre refinery to the Trinidadian government.[38]

In February 1984, the government appointed a team to begin negotiations with Texaco.[39] The Trinidadian government was interested in acquiring all of Texaco's assets in Trinidad, including Texaco's one-third share in the Trinidad Northern Areas consortium (TNA). Texaco, however, wanted to retain its share of this lucrative marine venture. The final agreement that was signed on March 30, 1985, allowed Texaco to retain its interests in TNA. The Trinidadian government acquired the Pointe-à-Pierre refinery, Texaco's land operations, and some real estate under Texaco's control. The total financial cost to the government was $189.2 million, of which $98 million was payable at the signing of the agreement, and the rest payable in oil over a ten-month period.[40]

The compensation package was very generous, particularly for assets that Texaco considered to be unprofitable. Many identified with the OWTU position that since the refinery was operating at a loss and since Texaco had no desire to continue operating it, Texaco should have offered the refinery to the government as a gesture of goodwill.[41] Moreover, the government already owned a refinery and was unable to provide the feedstocks necessary to keep it operating at full capacity. Further, the production from Texaco's land fields had been declining and only costly enhanced-recovery methods could produce additional oil. Given the declining price of oil, many felt that the lifting cost per barrel of oil could exceed the selling price of the same barrel of oil. Finally, many dismissed the government's claim that it had acquired land area "of a size most of you would never have imagined,"[42] because much of the real estate under Texaco's control had been leased to it by the Trinidadian government.[43]

Why did the host government acquire operations that a major oil-producing company regarded as unprofitable, and why on such generous terms? Texaco's threat in December of 1982 to close the Pointe-à-Pierre refinery took advantage of the government's vulnerability in two sensitive areas. Closure of the refinery would have meant the loss of about 4000 jobs and a major disruption in the commercial and social life in the oil belt, which was traditionally a pro-PNM area. The PNM government feared the political penalties it would have to pay for inaction. The next elections were just over a year away. Second, the domestic gasoline market was supplied by the Pointe-à-Pierre refinery. Closure would have caused a severe disruption in the domestic gasoline supply and hence a severe energy crisis in the country. Thus, Texaco's abrupt threat to close down the refinery forced the government to consider its purchase.[44]

The compensation for Texaco's assets was predictably generous. The PNM government had a record of being generous to departing companies. In this particular case, it feared the power of Texaco in the international oil market. It wanted to retain its image as a country hospitable to foreign enterprise, and a disgruntled Texaco would be damaging to this image. Finally, negotiations over the acquisition of Texaco's assets in Trinidad began in earnest in 1984 when relations between Trinidad and the United States were not very good. In October 1983, the Trinidadian government had refrained from participation in the U.S.-led invasion of Grenada and had criticized the action. Trinidad was also known to be a pro-OPEC country. The state of relations between the two countries was in the minds of the Trinidadian negotiators, and they did not want to incur the anger of the United States by any appearance of bullying a major U.S. company.[45] Texaco was thus able to unload its less profitable operations and to retain its share in the lucrative marine consortium, TNA.

TESORO'S DEPARTURE FROM TRINIDAD

On November 15, 1985, the government of Trinidad and Tobago acquired complete control of the Trinidad Tesoro Oil Company when it bought the shares of its minority partner, the Tesoro Petroleum Company of Texas. The government entered into negotiations with Tesoro after Tesoro had announced in May 1982 that it intended to liquidate its assets in Trinidad. By the articles of agreement signed in 1969, when the Trinidad Tesoro Oil Company was set up as a joint venture between Tesoro and the Trinidadian government, the latter had the right of first refusal.[46]

There were several reasons why Tesoro wanted to leave Trinidad. The first had to do with the 1981 change in the Trinidadian petroleum tax laws. The 1974 Petroleum Taxes Act had provided for profit calculations of the oil companies operating in Trinidad to be based on state-determined tax reference prices. The Trinidad Tesoro Oil Company was exempted from this law. Its tax liability, and hence Tesoro's tax liability in Trinidad, was computed on the basis of realized prices. This was easy to compute since the company sold the oil from its land fields to TRINTOC and its marine oil to Amoco. Tesoro was able to get a tax credit in the United States for the taxes it paid in Trinidad. The other U.S. oil companies operating in Trinidad complained that tax reference prices were arbitrary and were not recognized by the United States Internal Revenue Service. Hence, they could not get a tax credit in the United States for the taxes they paid in Trinidad. Moreover, the companies argued, the 1974 law was discriminatory and Tesoro's status was used as evidence. In 1981, the Trinidadian government bowed to pressure from the oil companies and amended the 1974 Petroleum Taxes Act to provide for the computation of the companies' tax obligations on the basis of actual prices. However, the law also provided for the Supplemental Petroleum Tax to be levied prior to the application of the Petroleum Profits Tax. Since the new law applied equally to the Trinidad Tesoro Oil Company, Tesoro lost the advantage it had relative to other U.S. oil companies, but more seriously, it was subject to greater annual tax liabilities. The company was not pleased. In its 1985 annual report, the company cited higher taxation as one of its reasons for selling.[47]

The second reason centered around policy differences between the two principal partners of the joint venture. It was agreed between the Trinidadian government and Tesoro, when the joint venture was established, that no dividends would be declared or paid to ordinary shareholders during the initial five years. After that initial period, if cash was available and if either party wanted it, 50 percent of net earnings after tax could be paid out as dividends. In 1981 and 1982, the board of directors of Trinidad Tesoro decided not to pay dividends, but to reinvest all of the profits into capital expansion. Tesoro was not happy with these decisions and demanded 50 percent of the profits in order to pay out dividends to its shareholders. The Trinidadian government firmly supported the reinvestment decision.[48] It must have appeared to Tesoro that these policy differences were likely to continue, given the declining trend in production in Trinidad and the natural need of its partner, the Trinidadian government, to want to engage in expensive enhanced-recovery methods and in new exploration.

However, the proximate cause of Tesoro's decision to leave Trinidad was the disgruntlement of its U.S. shareholders over the value of the company's stock. Some of Tesoro's shareholders were pressuring the company to come up with a plan to improve the value of the company's stock. In 1981, the value of the stock had dropped to $13 per share from a high of $25 per share. Shareholders were also criticizing the Tesoro management for turning down a 1980 offer by the Diamond Shamrock Corporation to buy the company for $32 a share. In response to these pressures, Tesoro's board drew up a plan to restructure the company. The plan involved a partial liquidation of some of Tesoro's operations and the formation of two new companies to handle the remainder of the business. The proceeds from the sales were to be distributed to the shareholders after the satisfaction of any liabilities. One of the operations earmarked for sale was Tesoro's 49.9 percent stake in the Trinidad Tesoro Oil Company.[49]

Tesoro demanded $200 million for its 49.9 percent equity in the Trinidad Tesoro Oil Company. The Trinidadian government initially countered with an offer of $50,000, arguing that this was Tesoro's initial investment and that while the company had not injected any new capital into the venture, it had already received $165 million in dividends. By making this counter-offer, the government was simply engaging in political posturing since it was aware of a large body of national sentiment favoring this amount. The government soon raised its counter-offer to $50 million. Since the two parties could not agree, the company's auditors were called in to determine the price. Provision for this was made in the articles of agreement that set up the joint venture.[50]

The price was to be based on the discounted value of future income up to the year 1997. A key element in projecting future income was the future price of oil. Tesoro projected a price increase while the government projected falling prices. The final price of Tesoro's assets was set in barrels of oil. For its share in the Trinidad Tesoro Oil Company, Tesoro received 3.2 million barrels of residual fuel oil to be delivered over an 18-month period beginning in May 1986.[51]

THE GOVERNMENT'S RELATIONS WITH AMOCO

The only major oil-producing company in Trinidad not under government control is Amoco. The PNM government had a special relationship with Amoco, which has been continued by the NAR government that took office in December 1986. No attempt has ever been made to buy into Amoco. In fact, the PNM government had entered into a joint venture with Amoco in establishing a fertilizer plant that utilizes natural gas produced by Amoco as feedstock.

Amoco's good relations with the government stem from the fact that during the 1960s when the oil situation in Trinidad was depressed, Amoco stuck with its oil lease until it discovered oil in 1968. Because of the large expenses involved in its offshore exploration, special concessions were given by the government under the Aid to Pioneer Industries ordinance. In interviews conducted by the author in 1982, senior officials in the Ministry of Energy recounted the numerous frustrations that Amoco experienced before it struck oil. The Ministry was constantly pleading with Amoco to stick with the exploration effort. The result was that when Amoco began commercial production, the government gave it a free hand.

Amoco is the largest producer of crude oil in Trinidad. The crude oil, which is produced from Amoco's offshore wells on the east coast of Trinidad, is of very high quality--high API gravity and low sulphur content. The oil is shipped directly to Amoco's refineries in the United States. The Petroleum Act of 1969 and the accompanying regulations require that a company producing 100,000 barrels of oil per day should construct an oil refinery in Trinidad. This requirement has not been invoked in the case of Amoco, even though Amoco's production rate has exceeded the stipulated 100,000 barrels per day since 1975. However, there already existed an excess of refinery capacity in Trinidad, and the PNM government was reluctant to increase the country's refinery capacity. That Amoco is not required to refine its oil locally is an anomaly. The explanation is that the local refineries are geared for low quality crude oil and that Amoco's crude oil fetches a higher price than the refined product of the local refineries. The PNM government accepted Amoco's participation in the joint venture for the production of fertilizers as a *quid pro quo* for relaxing the requirement of constructing a refinery.

A very significant feature of Amoco's operations is the fact that the oil union is not as firmly entrenched there as it is in the other companies. Amoco has structured its operations to require a minimum of labor, most of which is retained through contractors. Amoco has proved to be a good corporate citizen because it has filled its ranks with Trinidad nationals, and the general manager has always been someone who understands the conditions of operations in Third World countries. However, the most important point here is that because of the way Amoco has structured its operations, the OWTU does not have the same leverage there as it has elsewhere. The PNM government was happy with this situation, as is its successor, because Amoco's operations have been free of strikes and other labor-related disruptions in production. Further, without any significant foothold in Amoco's operations, the OWTU is less likely to be heeded in its calls for the nationalization of Amoco.

Amoco's production has been declining. It has not discovered any new oil fields. Its exploration activities have also declined. However, as former Minister of Energy Kelvin Ramnath explained, exploration off the east coast of Trinidad is very expensive, and, at a time of low oil prices, the oil companies are experiencing cash flow problems.[52] In fact, this was the argument of Robert Ridley, president of Amoco Trinidad Ltd., in calling for a reduction of the Supplemental Petroleum Tax (SPT) on marine production from 55 percent to 20 percent as an incentive to companies operating in Trinidad.[53] The NAR government was evidently persuaded since the SPT on marine production would be gradually reduced to 20 percent.[54]

MANAGING ECONOMIC NATIONALISM

Nationalizations by the PNM government occurred in a piecemeal fashion and against companies that were failing in Trinidad, so that these actions were in fact rescue operations. Even so, the government in each case negotiated a generous settlement with the departing company in order to preserve the image of the country as hospitable to foreign investors. At the same time, the government could use these acquisitions to appease domestic critics and to blunt the drive for the nationalization of the more successful oil companies, which, until 1982, were Texaco and Amoco. In this regard, the nationalization of the sugar industry paid significant political dividends because it contributed to the dismantling of an alliance between the oil and sugar unions.

The poor performance of state-run industries in the non-oil sector convinced both the PNM and the general populace that further nationalizations were likely to prove disastrous. Several state-owned companies such as Caroni Ltd., British West Indian Airways (BWIA), and the Iron Steel Company of Trinidad and Tobago (ISCOTT) were operating at a loss and needed to be heavily subsidized by the government to stay afloat. Of course, part of the reason for the poor performance of some of these state enterprises was the fact that at the time of nationalization, they were failing companies. Further, the fact that these companies could rely on state funding was a disincentive for efficient operation. Finally, these enterprises became a part of the ruling party's patronage system. Senior appointments within these enterprises were made on the basis of political rather than managerial criteria. Nevertheless, poor performance of state enterprises made people wary about further state ownership, especially of the oil industry, which had become the primary source of national prosperity. The PNM leadership could argue that there was no mandate for nationalization. Even the political opposition acknowledged this. One opposition leader, when asked whether he thought nationalization was a popular election issue, replied: "Nationalization as an issue has become discredited by the government. People get bored when the issue is raised. They think of BWIA, Caroni Ltd., etc., and the inefficiency, mismanagement, and corruption associated with it."[55]

The PNM was never motivated by any ideological commitment to nationalize. It took a pragmatic approach in its dealings with foreign enterprise. This meant exacting as much rent as possible from the companies without discouraging further investment. Only if a company began to cut back on employment and investment would the government intervene. Even in these circumstances, the government favored negotiation for some form of participation in order to inject the necessary capital to keep the enterprise going. The government would acquire the enterprise only if the owners were willing to sell. This was the approach it took with BP, Shell, Caroni Ltd., and later with Texaco and Tesoro.

There was also a political dimension to this pragmatism. In this regard, pragmatism meant doing the necessary minimum to mollify domestic radical groups and to prevent the mobilization of any mass-based coalition for further nationalization.

This chapter also shows that there was a relative strengthening of the host government's bargaining position vis-à-vis the oil multinationals largely as a result of exogenously determined increases in oil prices after 1973. The government ensured an increase in its share of the oil revenues by a manipulation of fiscal instruments. However, in 1981, the oil companies, by threatening to leave Trinidad, forced the government to revise the tax law in their favor. This shows that while a small mineral-producing country is interested in increasing its share of the revenues from the mineral industry, it also wants to ensure that it does not drive the multinationals away.

NOTES

1. Until his death in 1981, Eric Williams completely dominated the government of Trinidad. In 1970, for example, Williams was Prime Minister, Minister of Finance, Minister of Planning and Development, Minister of

Local Government, Minister of Tobago Affairs, and Minister of External Affairs. Although he subsequently relinquished some of these portfolios, he continued to dominate the government. See Selwyn D. Ryan, Race and Nationalism in Trinidad and Tobago: A Case Study of Decolonization in a Multiracial Society (Toronto: University of Toronto Press, 1972), p. 447.

2. OWTU, Oilfields Workers' Trade Union, p. 27.

3. Government of Trinidad and Tobago, Report of the Commission of Inquiry into the Oil Industry of Trinidad and Tobago, 1963-1964 (London: André Deutsch, 1964), p. 1.

4. Ibid., pp. 44, 46-62.

5. Cited in NACLA, "Oil in the Caribbean: Focus on Trinidad," Latin America and Empire Report 10 (October 1976), p. 25.

6. Carl D. Parris, Capital or Labour? The Decision to Introduce the Industrial Stabilization Act in Trinidad and Tobago, Working Paper No. 2 (Jamaica: Institute of Social and Economic Research, University of the West Indies, 1965), p. 30.

7. OWTU, Oil In Turmoil and OWTU Memorandum on the Formation of a National Oil Co. (San Fernando, Trinidad: Vanguard Publishing Company Ltd., 1967).

8. Ibid.

9. Ibid., pp. 9-10.

10. Trevor M.A. Farrell, "In Whose Interest: Nationalization and Bargaining with the Petroleum Multinationals: The Trinidad and Tobago Experience," in Proceedings of the Conference on Contemporary Trends and Issues in Caribbean International Affairs (St. Augustine, Trinidad: Institute of International Relations, University of the West Indies, 1977), p. 16.

11. Ibid., p. 17.

12. Ibid., pp. 18-19.

13. Ibid., p. 21.

14. Ibid., p. 22.

15. Vernetta Calvin-Smith, The Legal Regulations of Foreign Investment in the Petroleum Industry of Trinidad and Tobago (Port-of-Spain, Trinidad: Superservice Printing Company Limited, 1979), pp. 44-45.

16. Fourth Session Second Parliament Trinidad and Tobago, 18 Elizabeth II, Act No. 46 of 1969. See also "The Petroleum Regulations 1970," supplement to the Trinidad and Tobago Gazette 9 (February 19, 1970), p. 95.

17. Government of Trinidad and Tobago, Third Five-Year Plan 1969-1973 As Approved by Parliament (Port-of-Spain, Trinidad: The Government Printery, 1969), p. 31.

18. Ibid., p. 37.

19. See Eric Williams, Capitalism and Slavery (New York: Capricorn Books, 1966).

20. Caroni Limited, Directors' Reports and Accounts (Trinidad: Caroni Ltd., 1966 and 1967).

21. Trinidad Guardian, April 19, 1970, p. 1.

22. The situation was so serious that Eric Williams told his party convention on September 18, 1973, that he was considering resigning his office as Prime Minister. See "Address by Mr. Karl T. Hudson-Phillips at the

Inauguration of the Organization for National Reconstruction on Sunday lst February, 1981, at the Chaguaramas Convention Centre," pp. 12-15.

23. Cited in Ryan, Race and Nationalism, p. 426.

24. Trinidad Guardian, December 4, 1973, p. 1.

25. Interview, Trinidad and Tobago Oil Company, Port-of-Spain, Trinidad, March 18, 1982.

26. Third Session Third Parliament Trinidad and Tobago, 23 Elizabeth II, Act No. 22 of 1974. See also Calvin-Smith, The Legal Regulations, p. 105.

27. Trevor M.A. Farrell, "The Multinational Corporations, the Petroleum Industry and Economic Underdevelopment in Trinidad and Tobago," Ph.D. dissertation, Cornell University, 1974, pp. 204-210.

28. See "An Act to Amend the Petroleum Taxes Act, 1974," speech by the Minister of Energy and Energy-based Industries, Second Reading of the Bill, April 22, 1981.

29. "Trinidad," World Oil 191 (August 15, 1980), p. 123.

30. Fifth Session First Parliament Republic of Trinidad and Tobago, Act No. 5 of 1981.

31. Trinidad Guardian, January 25, 1976, p. 1.

32. Trinidad Guardian, June 6, 1976, p. 1.

33. "Govt. Team to look into Texaco's future," Trinidad Guardian (July 3, 1983), p. 1.

34. Ibid.

35. Mickey Mahabir, "Texaco Gives a Deadline," Trinidad Guardian (December 7, 1982), p. 1.

36. Budget Speech 1984 of The Honourable George M. Chambers, Prime Minister and Minister of Finance and Planning, Wednesday, 11th January, 1984 (Trinidad: Government Printing, 1984), p. 22.

37. Ibid., p. 7.

38. Ibid., p. 22.

39. "Government To Negotiate With Texaco," Express (February 3, 1984), p. 1.

40. Camini Marajh, "Texaco Is Ours," Sunday Express (March 31, 1985), pp. 1, 3. See also John Babb, "Goodbye Texaco, hello Trintoc," Sunday Guardian (March 31, 1985), pp. 1, 12.

41. "Texaco Value Put at $302M," Trinidad Guardian (December 22, 1983), p. 1.

42. "Gov't Buys Out Texaco," Express (August 31, 1984), p. 1.

43. Interview with Kelvin Ramnath, former Minister of Energy (January 1987 - March 1988), in New York City, May 7, 1988.

44. Interview, August 19, 1987.

45. Ibid.

46. Norris Solomon, "Tesoro Talks Opening Today," Trinidad Guardian (September 28, 1982), p. 1; "Talks open on purchase of Tesoro shares," Express (September 27, 1982), p. 1; "$200M for $50,000 investment boasts Tesoro," Sunday Guardian (February 23, 1986), p. 1.

47. Solomon, "$200M for $50,000 Investment," p. 1.

48. "Tesoro Threat: "Pay dividends or else...," Sunday Guardian (March 23, 1983), p. 1.

20

49. Alexander R. Hammer, "Tesoro Petroleum Plans A Major Restructuring," <u>New York Times</u> (May 28, 1982) Section D, p. 3; "Tesoro Studies Plan to Sell Some Assets, Spin Off Remainder," <u>Wall Street Journal</u>, May 28, 1982, p. 4.

50. Andy Johnson, "Govt. At A Standstill In The Tesoro Deal," <u>Express</u> (October 12, 1982), p. 1; "Govt. expected to offer Tesoro $50M," <u>Express</u> (October 19, 1982), p. 13; Raoul Pantin, "Now a new twist in Tesoro Talks," <u>Sunday Express</u> (October 17, 1983), pp. 3, 21; "The Marriage with Tesoro," <u>Sunday Guardian</u> (September 9, 1984), p. 6.

51. Michael G. Toney, "Tesoro Shares--for how much?" <u>Trinidad Guardian</u> (November 27, 1985), p. 9; Norris Solomon, "$200M for $50,000 Investment," p. 1.

52. Interview with Kelvin Ramnath, May 7, 1988.

53. The author observed an interview with Robert Ridley, president of Amoco, on Trinidad and Tobago Television (TTT) on August 12, 1987. This edition of TTT's "The Money Programme" was entitled "Amoco's Future--A Taxing Question," and was aired at 8:00 p.m. local time.

54. Interview with Kelvin Ramnath, May 7, 1988.

55. Interview, Port-of-Spain, Trinidad, February 26, 1987.

7 CONCLUSION

A SUMMARY OF THE TRINIDADIAN CASE STUDY

This study has focused principally on the relationship between the Trinidadian government and the foreign investors in the oil industry. It examines how the size of Trinidad's oil reserves has restricted the options available to the government in its dealings with the oil multinationals. The study also examines how the role of foreign investors in oil and sugar became an issue of domestic politics, and how domestic politics impinged on the government's relations with the foreign companies. The principal arguments will now be summarized.

It is clear that, based on the petroleum sector's contribution to GDP, to total exports, and to government revenues, the Trinidadian economy is highly dependent on this sector. As a result of the OPEC price regime in effect after 1973, all of these indicators rose, especially the contribution of the petroleum sector to GDP and to the government revenues. Increased revenues from this sector allowed the government to maintain a number of state enterprises and to heavily subsidize the standard of living of the Trinidadian people. Because of the essentiality of petroleum to the economy, the government was reluctant to take any action that might have resulted in a disruption of the flow of these revenues.

Although by the mid-1970s the government of Trinidad enjoyed a significant presence in the oil industry by virtue of its ownership of one oil company and its controlling interest in another, the industry continued to be dominated by the foreign companies Amoco and Texaco. The government was heavily dependent on the foreign companies in all phases of the industry. Trinidadians have had much greater experience in land production. However, the shift in emphasis from land to marine production has created a technological gap in the Trinidadian oil industry because marine production requires technological expertise that is unavailable locally in Trinidad. The result is that Trinidad continues to rely on foreign companies, primarily

Amoco in this case, to provide the expertise or to manage the expertise where Amoco has itself rented it.

Moreover, to maintain its position as a refining center, Trinidad required feedstocks of crude oil in larger quantities than were available locally. Until 1982, it was able to secure these through Texaco, which not only brought in crude oil from its subsidiaries in other parts of the world, but also marketed the products through its outlets in the United States. This made the government of Trinidad very dependent on Texaco. After Texaco's departure in 1985, the government controlled the refining component of the industry, but the scale of operations was considerably reduced.

In the area of marketing, the government recognized the usefulness of its relations with the multinational corporations. Amoco and Texaco marketed their petroleum and petroleum products. Trinidad Tesoro sold the crude oil from its land fields to the state-owned company TRINTOC, and its marine-produced oil to Amoco. The poor performance of the state-owned company in the U.S. market vindicated the wisdom of retaining the marketing outlets of the foreign companies.

The government also depended heavily on foreign companies in the exploration for oil, the area that has the greatest risk. The PNM government recognized that it could ill afford the capital outlay such activity required and that it did not have the expertise or the experience that the major oil companies had developed.

Given the great dependence of the country on the foreign companies in all stages of the oil industry, it is one of the conclusions of this study that, from an economic point of view, the nationalization of these companies never made sense. Moreover, the early industrialization plan envisaged a central role for foreign investors, and the government feared that nationalization would destroy the reputation of the country as having an investment climate that was hospitable to foreign investors. In fact, considerations about creating a stable investment climate dovetailed with domestic political reasons for imposing controls over the activities of organized labor.

Despite the fact that the government spoke of its interest in controlling the commanding heights of the economy, it outlined no comprehensive plan to bring this about. This goal must be seen as an attempt to placate its domestic supporters and mollify its critics. The actual behavior of the PNM government toward foreign investors suggests that the government was content to exact rent through fiscal means, though it preferred equity participation if this could be negotiated.

The preceding suggests a government with a fairly constricted set of options insofar as its dealings with the multinationals were concerned. For a long time the government was able to keep these dealings insulated from domestic politics. In fact, the ruling party in Trinidad had reason to assume that its continuation in office would not be affected by its dealings with the MNCs, because such issues were of only secondary importance in Trinidadian politics.

As argued in Chapter 4, ethnicity is the dominant variable of political life in Trinidad. The PNM's protracted stay in power was based on a strategy of presenting itself as the defender of the interests of the black and mixed-black majority. In this setting, all other issues or policies were relegated to a secondary position. Between 1961 and 1974, dissension and fragmentation within the parliamentary opposition party rendered it ineffective, and the PNM government was relieved of an important source of domestic pressure.

However, the challenge to governmental relations with the oil multinationals came from other quarters. The oil union leadership, which has always been prominent within the Trinidad left, recognized that the only way it could pose a serious challenge to the PNM government was to build an inter-ethnic coalition between the black working class located in the oil belt and the Indian working class in the sugar belt. The strategy was to submerge ethnic differences by emphasizing common class interests. The foreign companies in the oil and sugar industries were portrayed as exploiters of the black and Indian working classes. The call for the nationalization of these foreign companies was central to a mobilization strategy aimed at bridging the ethnic gap between black oil workers and Indian sugar workers.

The oil union leadership tried to bring both groups of workers under its control in 1965, but this attempt did not succeed. Instead, the government used the occasion to isolate the oil union by alleging communist infiltration of that organization, and to impose anti-strike legislation in the form of the Industrial Stabilization Act. The oil union later used the Black Power demonstrations of 1970 to press its call for the nationalization of the oil and sugar industries, and to emphasize the need for unity between blacks and Indians. The government succumbed to pressure for nationalization, but chose the sugar industry. The sugar industry was losing money and the owners wanted to unload it. Two years later, the government strengthened its control over organized labor by the enactment of the Industrial Relations Act, which prevented any union from organizing and representing workers in two or more "essential" industries.

The fragmentation of the parliamentary opposition party, the DLP, created a political vacuum that was filled by a leftist coalition consisting primarily of union leaders. In 1975, the oil and sugar unions, allied with the transportation workers' union, established the United Labor Front. The original idea was to present a common front in pressing their respective wage demands against the foreign companies. The organization grew into a political party, the ULF. One of its principal demands was the nationalization of both the oil and sugar industries.

The ULF's impressive performance in the 1976 election caused the PNM government to fear this coalition. Consequently, it took the nationalization demand very seriously. It moved to complete the nationalization of the sugar industry and initiated talks with Texaco on the question of equity participation in that company. However, the threat from the ULF began to dissipate as the party became torn by ideological differences. After 1977, the party became ineffective as a parliamentary opposition. Relieved of this source of domestic pressure and encountering resistance from Texaco, the government did not press its demand for equity participation in Texaco. Instead, it chose to use fiscal measures to maximize its share of the revenues from the industry.

In 1985, the PNM government acquired Texaco's land operations and refinery and Tesoro's shares in the Trinidad Tesoro Oil Company. Both Texaco and Tesoro were willing sellers. Both saw a bleak future for oil production in Trinidad, and Texaco wanted to terminate its refining operations as well. Texaco pressured the government into the purchase of the refinery by abruptly terminating imports of crude oil. The prospect of massive unemployment in the oil belt and a domestic gasoline shortage forced the government to enter into negotiations with Texaco with a view to purchasing Texaco's assets in Trinidad.

Thus national ownership of foreign companies was neither dictated by a comprehensive plan nor motivated by the prospect of financial gain. National ownership occurred in piecemeal fashion in response to various domestic crises. The companies over which the government secured control projected future losses if they remained in the country and their owners wanted to unload them. This was certainly the case of British Petroleum in 1969 and of Shell in 1974, and eventually of Texaco and Tesoro. However, until 1982, the government refused to consider the nationalization of Texaco and Amoco, despite strident demands for the nationalization of the entire oil industry. Against this background, the nationalization of the sugar industry was a master stroke by the PNM government.

The domestic groups in favor of nationalization of foreign companies made a combined call for the nationalization of the oil and sugar companies. Since the sugar industry was losing money, buying into the sugar company was not in any way threatening to foreign investors. In 1970, in response to the Black Power call for nationalization, the government bought 51 percent of the ordinary shares in Caroni Ltd. However, when the crisis subsided, the government backed off from further action against any of the companies in oil and sugar. In 1975, when the United Labor Front called for the nationalization of the oil and sugar industries, the government proceeded to complete the nationalization of the sugar industry, but the oil industry was left intact. Again, the government showed that it was responding to nationalistic demands, but it chose a company that wanted to unload its assets.

The nationalization of the sugar industry contributed to the fragmentation of the United Labor Front. The subsidization of the sugar industry by the government set the stage for a more collaborative relationship between the government and the leadership of the sugar union. The continued injection of capital into the sugar industry depended on the uninterrupted flow of revenues from the oil industry. And the sugar union softened its position on the issue of nationalization of the oil industry. By nationalizing the sugar industry first, the government drove a wedge between the leadership of the sugar union and that of the oil union and blunted the overall drive for the nationalization of the oil industry.

The nationalizations that took place in the oil and sugar industries between 1970 and 1975 and the control imposed on organized labor amounted to an effort on the part of the PNM government to manage economic nationalism in the country. The PNM government had no intention of completely nationalizing the oil industry, which was recognized as the "golden goose" of the economy. In its dealings with the multinationals in the oil industry, the government's principal goal was to exact the maximum amount of revenues without driving the companies away.

The first move in this direction was the enactment of the Petroleum Act of 1969. In addition to a modest increase in the fiscal obligations of the companies, the law reduced the submarine depletion allowance from 20 to 10 percent of the gross value of production. What motivated this change was the large oil discovery by Amoco off the east coast of Trinidad in 1968 and the expectation of increased drilling activity in submarine areas thereafter. However, the major renegotiation of the government's position with the oil companies occurred after the OPEC price increase in 1973. The government rewrote the petroleum tax law in 1974 in order to take advantage of this windfall. The justification offered by the government was that it was merely following an international precedent; it was asking from the oil companies no more than they were required to pay elsewhere. In addition, the government required any company beginning exploration and production operations after November 1, 1974, to enter into a production-sharing contract with the government. Again, this move was consistent with similar arrangements taking place elsewhere. Governments did not want to get into the very expensive exploration business but wanted to benefit from the discoveries.

The oil companies were not happy with the tax regime established by the 1974 Petroleum Taxes Act and lobbied hard for a change. Their bargaining position was strengthened by the fact that petroleum production in Trinidad was declining after 1978, and the trend was expected to continue unless new discoveries were made. To apply pressure on the government, the companies slowed down their exploration and drilling activities and in general demonstrated a lack of interest in continuing their operations in Trinidad. This tacit threat to abandon Trinidad alarmed the government, and it acceded to the companies' demand for a change in the Petroleum Taxes Act of 1974. The result was a new system of taxation that was much more favorable to the oil companies. Faced with the possibility of a withdrawal by the companies, the government yielded to their demands, and in May 1981, a new system of petroleum taxation was enacted and made retroactive to January 1, 1980. Here we see that while the government was interested in increasing its share of the oil revenues, it was also interested in keeping the companies operating in the country. However, these concessions were not enough to keep Texaco and Tesoro.

TRINIDAD AS A SMALL MINERAL-PRODUCING COUNTRY

In Chapter 1 a model was proposed which represents the relations between the government of a small mineral-producing country and the multinationals involved in the extraction of the mineral, and also the interpenetration of those relations and the domestic politics of the country. We will now examine how the Trinidadian case fits the set of propositions embodied in the model:

1. Whether a marginal source of raw materials is developed or not depends on the essentiality of the commodity to the advanced industrialized countries.

2. Unlike the case of a country with large reserves, the foreign investor in a small mineral-producing country can manipulate the existence of risk in its operations to keep the host government's bargaining position weak.

3. The small size of the mineral reserves adversely affects the development of indigenous expertise in the exploration, production, and marketing of the mineral.

4. It follows from proposition 3 that the host country's initial dependence on the foreign investor's technological, managerial, and marketing expertise is likely to be maintained for the duration of the concession agreement and that nationalization of the foreign investor is not a feasible option.

5. Nationalization as a host-government option is also deterred by the following considerations:
   (i)   the cost of compensation as compared with the expected flow of profits from the industry under conditions of local ownership and management;
   (ii) developmental pressures and the need for a steady stream of revenue from the mineral industry;
   (iii) the vulnerability of the host government to sanctions from the foreign investor's home government, as well as from the international investing community.

6. The threat by the foreign company to abandon its operations in the short term is much more potent against the small mineral-producing country than it is against a major producer.

7. In its bargaining with the multinational corporation, the host government of a small mineral-production country is motivated by two principal goals:
   (i)   to try to increase its share of the revenues generated by the mineral industry;
   (ii) to keep the multinational operating in the country.

8. As the foreign-controlled industry increases in importance to the economy, that is, as the size of its contribution to the economy increases, it will become more and more of an issue of domestic politics. The ability of the host government to achieve its principal goals, outlined in proposition 7, will depend on its ability to manage its domestic politics.

The first proposition receives mixed support on the basis of the evidence generated from the Trinidad case study. There is no doubt that Trinidad is a marginal source of petroleum. In the early 1960s, two companies, British Petroleum and Shell, were preparing to leave Trinidad. They argued that declining production and poor prospects for new discoveries made Trinidad unattractive for future oil investment. Yet during the same time period, Amoco, a relatively new company in Trinidad, was intensifying its exploration efforts off the coast of Trinidad. Amoco eventually made a major oil discovery in 1968. Since that time, other companies have been conducting exploration for oil in Trinidad (see Chapter 3). Even though Trinidad is a marginal source of petroleum, the essentiality of this commodity to the advanced industrialized countries has ensured that this marginal source will be fully tapped.

The evidence from the Trinidadian case substantiates the second proposition. This study has shown that until 1973 the bargaining strength of the government vis-à-vis the oil companies was very weak. After 1973, however, the new role assumed by the major producing countries strengthened the Trinidadian government relative to the foreign oil companies operating in the country. The government seized this opportunity to renegotiate its position with the oil companies, and the readjustment was reflected in the Petroleum Taxes Act of 1974. The foreign oil companies were not happy with the new tax system and lobbied for a change. In order to pressure the government to change the law, the companies began to manipulate the existence of risk in their operations by slowing down their exploration and drilling activities. They were successful in this overall effort because most of the early seismic studies and exploration work were conducted by the foreign oil companies and the data have not been independently checked by the government. Eventually, the government changed the petroleum tax system to make it more favorable to the companies.

Propositions 3 and 4 are strongly supported by this study. Public perception of the industry as short-lived made it unattractive as a career opportunity for large numbers of university students. The result is that within Trinidad there exists a shortage of petroleum engineers, petroleum inspectors, and geologists (see Chapter 3). Two developments in petroleum production in Trinidad have accentuated the deficiency in indigenous expertise. First, declining land production required the use of enhanced-recovery methods. Second, the shift in emphasis from land to offshore production required a new form of technology. Neither the skills in enhanced-recovery methods nor those in marine exploration and production were available locally in Trinidad. Thus the country's dependence on the foreign companies was maintained.

The Trinidadian government did not become involved in marketing until it nationalized Shell in 1974. Thereafter, the Shell assets were operated by the state-owned company TRINTOC. The poor performance of TRINTOC in the marketing of its products outside of the Caribbean alerted the government to the enormousness of the marketing problems it would face if it nationalized the entire industry. The result was a further dependence on the foreign companies. And given this continuing dependence on the foreign companies for technological and marketing skills, nationalization of the oil industry has not been a realistic option.

Proposition 5 is also supported by the Trinidadian case study. The Trinidadian government never attempted to acquire equity in Amoco. The cost of a producing company like Amoco could run into billions of dollars, and the government could not afford this, especially in light of the bleak future of the industry.

Also, as discussed in Chapter 2, the state heavily subsidizes a large number of public enterprises, as well as the standard of living of the general population. Its ability to continue this role depends on the steady flow of revenues from the oil industry. There was, and continues to be, a strong reluctance on the part of the government to take against the foreign oil companies any action that would result in a disruption of the flow of these revenues. Given the country's dependence on the foreign oil companies, nationalization has been seen as likely to result in a disruption in the flow of revenues to the government and has therefore not been a popular consideration.

Trinidad's vulnerability to pressure from the home government of the multinationals was demonstrated in 1976 during the government's negotiations with Texaco over the question of equity participation in the company. The U.S. ambassador to Trinidad publicly exerted pressure on the Trinidadian government and the latter succumbed. Moreover, in its dealing with both the foreign investors in the country and organized labor, the government of Trinidad tried to build a reputation for the country as one that provided a stable investment climate. Actions against the multinationals that might have been perceived as radical by prospective investors were carefully avoided.

Support for proposition 6 can be inferred from the behavior of the Trinidadian government in those instances when foreign oil companies were actually withdrawing or seemed to be withdrawing. In 1969, when British Petroleum offered its assets in Trinidad for sale, the government panicked. It tried to persuade British Petroleum to stay. When this failed, it tried to get Shell and Texaco to buy British Petroleum's assets, but these companies declined. The government then purchased those assets in a joint-venture arrangement with Tesoro of Texas. Tesoro was able to exploit the government's state of panic to obtain exceptionally generous terms. Further, in the late 1970s the oil companies demanded a change in the petroleum tax system and backed up this demand by a curtailment in exploration and drilling activities. The government feared that the companies might be preparing to withdraw from the country and acceded to their demands in the hope of keeping them operating in the country. These threats, that is, threats of withdrawing from the host country, have not been reported in any of the studies of major mineral-producing countries, for example, in the cases of copper in Chile and of oil in Venezuela. In fact, conflict arose in those cases because the host governments wanted the foreign companies to leave whereas the latter wanted to remain.

The preceding discussion supports the claim in proposition 7 that one of the principal goals of the host government of a small mineral-producing country is to keep the multinational operating in the country. The Petroleum Act of 1969 and the 1974 Petroleum Taxes Act contributed to the achievement of the host-government's other goal, that is, to try to increase its share of the oil revenues. Although the 1981 Petroleum Taxes Act was a capitulation to the oil companies, the government ensured that it continued to get a sizable share of the revenues resulting from high oil prices.

Finally, support for proposition 8 can be inferred from the action taken by the government of Trinidad to ward off the nationalization of

Texaco and Amoco in the 1970s. The cumulative effect of all of the actions taken by the government against domestic labor, and the nationalization of British Petroleum, Shell, and Caroni Ltd., had been to manage economic nationalism in the country.

DEPENDENCY, BARGAINING, AND THE TRINIDAD CASE STUDY

In this section, we will examine the empirical fit of the Trinidad case study with the dependency and bargaining models discussed in Chapter 1. We will show that although the Trinidadian case study is illustrative of some of the propositions identified with the Marxist dependency approach and the bargaining model proposed by Theodore Moran, it diverges from these models in one major respect; that is, it suggests that for a small mineral-producing country, nationalization of the entire mineral industry is virtually foreclosed as a viable economic option.

As noted in Chapter 1, the Marxist dependency model views the multinational corporation as a mechanism by which center countries exploit the economies of periphery countries. Corporate decision-making is centralized in the home country of the multinational and is preoccupied with global profit maximization. The multinational's decision-making reflects its insensitivity to the developmental priorities of the periphery countries in which it operates. When the minerals of a periphery country are exhausted or when the market for its agricultural commodities disappears, the multinational corporation will abandon the developing country to its own devices.

Based on the above considerations, the Trinidadian case study fits the dependency model very well. In 1965, Texaco's chairman of the board pointed out the global emphasis of the company's planning (see Chapter 6). He wanted to make Trinidadian officials understand that Texaco could increase or decrease its production and refining capacity at will, regardless of what happened in the Trinidad oil industry. During the same year, the multinationals rebuffed the efforts of the government to enlist their active collaboration in broadening the country's economic base by establishing backward and forward linkages with the oil and sugar industries, thereby demonstrating their lack of concern about the development of the host country.

Further, when the oil reserves in Trinidad appeared to be dwindling, some of the oil multinationals began to pull out. British Petroleum left in 1969, and Shell sold its assets to the Trinidadian government in 1974. This pattern was also true in agribusiness. As profits began to fall in the sugar industry, the British multinational company Tate and Lyle began to contemplate unloading its assets and finally sold out to the government in 1975. In 1985, Texaco and Tesoro pulled out under similar circumstances. Thus far, the Trinidadian case study fits in with the predictions of the dependency model.

However, the dependency approach advocates the nationalization of the foreign companies by the periphery country as an essential part of the overall effort to rupture the structure of dependency, and this recommendation poses serious problems for a small mineral-producing country such as Trinidad. The dependency approach does not elaborate on the prospects for long-term development in the case of a marginal mineral economy that has nationalized its mineral industry. This case study, on the other hand, shows that Trinidad cannot draw on indigenous expertise to replicate the range of services currently being provided by the multinationals.

The Trinidadian case study highlights two other deficiencies of dependency theory. First, dependency theory underestimates the ability of periphery countries to alter the terms of exchange with center countries and with the latter's intermediaries, the multinational corporations. The countries in the OPEC cartel were phenomenally successful in this regard, and even marginal petroleum producers such as Trinidad benefited. In fact, after 1973, the Trinidadian government was successful in renegotiating its position with the oil multinationals.

The other deficiency of dependency theory is that this theory underestimates the ability of the periphery country to promote its own development. In the case of Trinidad, the government used the windfall revenues from the oil industry to expand its industrial infrastructure to include several petrochemical industries and an iron and steel factory. Contrary to dependency theory, therefore, foreign investment has not, on balance, been detrimental to the development of Trinidad.

The bargaining model proposed by Theodore Moran predicts a cumulative shift of bargaining power from the multinational to the host country. The shift is due to the ability of the host country to develop the indigenous expertise that would put it in a position to dispense with the services of the multinational altogether. The Trinidad case can be seen as a special application of the bargaining model.

The initial resource endowment position of the country was small, and so its initial bargaining position vis-à-vis the multinationals was weak. However, because its reserves position was never substantially upgraded compared with other oil-producing countries, the country's bargaining position remained weak.

Further, the country's dependence on the multinationals for technical, managerial, and marketing expertise has been maintained. It is unlikely that the country will develop the full complement of indigenous expertise before the resource is exhausted. This constrains the host government to pursue two principal goals: to try to increase its share of the revenues from the industry while providing the multinationals with sufficient inducements to keep them producing. Under these circumstances, the threat by a multinational to withdraw from the country is potent and can be used to force concessions from the host government, as illustrated by the Trinidadian case study.

While there has been no cumulative shift in bargaining power to the Trinidadian government, the latter has experienced some improvement in its position. In 1970, with a mob at its heels, the Trinidadian government was able to increase the corporation tax that the foreign companies pay. In 1973, the government's position was also strengthened by the actions taken by OPEC. The government was able to achieve substantial gains by an overhaul of the petroleum tax system in Trinidad. However, in 1981, the government was forced to make concessions to the foreign oil companies which gave the impression that they would leave if these concessions were not forthcoming. Thus shifts in the bargaining power between the oil companies and the Trinidadian government are more accurately described as oscillatory, in contrast to the cumulative shifts predicted by the bargaining model.

Finally, both of these models, the dependency and the Moran bargaining models, suggest that nationalization might maximize the gains to the host government at some point. The Trinidadian case study has shown that for a small mineral-producing country, nationalization is not a prudent economic option.

WIDER APPLICABILITY OF THE TRINIDADIAN CASE STUDY

This study has examined the opportunities available to a small mineral-producing country to improve its bargaining position with the multinationals involved in the mineral industry. Trinidad, as a small petroleum producer, has been used as an illustrative case study. The question that arises is: To what extent is Trinidad typical of the small mineral-producing country whose economy is highly dependent on the export of its mineral?

Three factors determine the nature of host government-MNC relations and the interpenetration of these relations and domestic politics. These factors are: the small resource-endowment position of the host country; the size of the contribution that the foreign-dominated mineral industry makes to the economy; and international market conditions as reflected in the price of the mineral.

The small size of the country's mineral reserves determines the range of possible outcomes of the bargaining that takes place between the host government and the MNC. It explains why host-country dependence on the MNC for technological, managerial, and marketing expertise is likely to be maintained for the duration of the concessions agreement. It explains why nationalization of the MNC is not a prudent economic option for the host government.

However, nationalizations are not always motivated by the prospect of economic gain. Domestic political pressures can cause a government to demand from the MNC more than its true bargaining position warrants or than economic prudence dictates. What makes the foreign-controlled mineral industry an issue of domestic politics is the size of its contribution to the host country's economy. As the size of this contribution increases, the visibility of the foreign companies increases. If the foreign-controlled mineral industry dominates the economy, it will attract the attention of domestic opposition groups, some of which will try to increase their domestic support by advocating more nationalistic positions vis-à-vis the foreign companies. Thus the factor that decides the degree to which the host government-MNC relations intersect with the domestic politics of the country is the size of the contribution that the mineral industry makes to the economy. These two factors, the small size of the country's mineral reserves and the size of the mineral sector's contribution to the economy, affect all small mineral-producing countries similarly.

The third factor, the world market price of the mineral, determines whether or not the host government can make improvements in its share of the revenues. An increase in the world market price of the commodity allows the government the opportunity to increase its share of the revenues. A drop in the world market price could force the government to accept a smaller proportion of the revenues. The world market price also affects the size of the contribution that the mineral industry makes to the economy. An increase in the size of this contribution increases the visibility of the foreign companies in the industry and increases the probability that host government-MNC relations would become a major issue of domestic politics.

It could be argued that Trinidad is different from most other small mineral-producing countries because of the nature of its mineral: petroleum. This is partly true. Petroleum has proven to be more suitable for cartelization than most other commodities, and as a result, fetches a much higher price per unit. Thus while price fluctuations of other commodities tend to be the norm, petroleum prices have been kept high for an extended period of time and will probably remain high. Yet if we examined the case of Trinidad prior to the 1973 petroleum price increases (see especially Tables 2.4 and 2.5), we will find that the petroleum industry dominated the economy then. Moreover, the role of the foreign companies in that industry had already become a major issue of domestic politics. After 1973, increased oil revenues increased the visibility of the foreign oil companies. The basic argument of this book is therefore not significantly altered by the fact that Trinidad is a petroleum producer, and its applicability extends to other small mineral-producing countries whose economic well-being depends on their mineral sectors.

APPENDIX

INTERVIEWS WITH AUTHOR (1982)

Abdullah, David, Research and Education Officer, OWTU
Ali, Basharat, National Energy Corporation
Barnes, Barry, Marketing Officer, TRINTOC
Barsotti, Frank, Permanent Secretary, Ministry of Finance; chairman of the
    Board of Directors, Caroni Ltd.
Beraux, H.S.K., legal adviser, Trinidad Tesoro Oil Company
Best, Lloyd, Senator, leader of TAPIA
Best, Winston, administrative officer of the Party Secretariat, PNM
Bisoondath, C., production manager, Trinidad Tesoro Oil Company
Boopsingh, Trevor, Permanent Secretary, Ministry of Energy
Bruce, N., professor and head of the Petroleum Engineering Department,
    UWI; consultant to the government on oil matters
DaSilva, Vernon, tax officer, Ministry of Energy
Davis, Stephen, Senior Reservoir Engineer, Ministry of Energy
Defreitas, Rodney, director, Santa Fe Drilling Company
Diaz, Nuevo, vice-president, ATSEFWTU
Fernandes, Ovid, senior petroleum adviser, Ministry of Energy
Gilbert, Vernon, chief petroleum engineer, Trinidad Tesoro Oil Company
Haraksingh, Kusha, lecturer, UWI; former ULF Senator
Harinanan, Austin, Director of Economic and Industrial Research at the
    Industrial Court
Hudson-Phillips, Karl T., leader of the Organization for National
    Reconstruction; former Attorney General of Trinidad
Layne, Lugard, petroleum engineer, Trinidad Tesoro Oil Company
Lequay, Alloy, Former Leader of the DLP
Lookin, Frank, Assistant Chief Petroleum Engineer, Ministry of Energy
Maharaj, Jainarine, Research and Education Officer, Trinidad Labor
    Congress

Manning, Patrick, Minister of Energy
Marshall, Max, Officer of Government Relations, Texaco
Mends, Rupert, National Energy Corporation
Mohammed, Kamaluddin, Minister of Agriculture
Morris, Oswald, executive director of the Trinidad and Tobago Chamber of
    Commerce; public relations officer, Texaco (on leave)
Panday, Basdeo, opposition leader; leader of the ULF; president of the
    ATSEFWTU
Pantin, Anthony, Archbishop of Trinidad and Tobago
Pierre, Lennox, legal adviser, OWTU; former leader of the WIIP
Ramlakhan, Tensingh, petroleum inspector, Ministry of Energy
Ramlogan, Vishnu, lecturer, UWI; former ULF Senator
Rampersad, Frank, president, NIHERST
Renwick, David, journalist, former editor of Express
Robinson, A.N.R., leader, Democratic Action Congress; former Deputy
    Prime Minister
Rogers, Val, consultant to the Chamber of Commerce on Trade and
    Development
Sahadeo, Indar, lecturer, Cipriani Labor College
Singh, Rampartap, former president, ATSEFWTU
Singh, Ranjit, UWI lecturer; member of the Board of Directors, Caroni Ltd.
Sudama, Trevor, member of Parliament, ULF
Walrond, Kermit, operations manager, Amoco

INTERVIEWS WITH AUTHOR (1987-1988)

Abdullah, David, Research and Education Officer, OWTU
Boopsingh, Trevor, Permanent Secretary, Ministry of Labor; former
    Permanent Secretary, Minister of Energy
Fernandes, Ovid, former senior petroleum adviser, Ministry of Energy
Manning, Patrick, leader of the opposition; leader of the PNM; former
    Minister of Energy
Mootoo, Winston, member of the Board of Directors, TRINTOC
Panday, Basdeo, Minister of External Affairs
Ramnath, Kelvin, former Minister of Energy
Tewarie, Beauendradat, General Secretary, NAR
Tiwary, Sais, member of the Board of Directors, TRINTOC

BIBLIOGRAPHY

BOOKS

Akinsanya, Adeoye A. Multinationals in a Changing Environment. New York: Praeger Publishers, 1984.

Apter, David E., and L.W. Goodman, eds. The Multinational Corporation and Social Change. New York: Praeger Publishers, 1976.

Arad, Ruth W., and Uzi B. Arad. "Scarce Natural Resources and Potential Conflict," in Ruth W. Arad et al., Sharing Global Resources. New York: McGraw-Hill, 1979.

Bahadoorsingh, Krishna. Trinidad Electoral Politics: The Persistence of the Race Factor. London: Institute of Race Relations, 1968.

Baptiste, Owen, ed. Crisis. Trinidad: Inprint Caribbean Ltd., 1976.

Barnet, Richard J., and Ronald E. Muller. Global Reach: The Power of the Multinational Corporations. New York: Simon and Schuster, 1974.

Bhagwati, Jagdish N., ed. The New International Economic Order: The North-South Debate. Cambridge, Mass.: MIT Press, 1977.

Biersteker, Thomas J. Multinationals, the State, and Control of the Nigerian Economy. Princeton: Princeton University Press, 1987.

Black, Jan Knippers, et al. Area Handbook for Trinidad and Tobago. Washington, D.C.: American University, 1976.

Brereton, Bridget. A History of Modern Trinidad. London: Heineman Educational Books Ltd., 1981.

Calvin-Smith, Vernetta. The Legal Regulations of Foreign Investment in the Petroleum Industry of Trinidad and Tobago. Port-of-Spain, Trinidad: Superservice Printing Company Limited, 1979.

Cardoso, Fernando Henrique. "Associated-Dependent Development: Theoretical and Practical Implications," in Alfred Stepan, ed., Authoritarian Brazil. New Haven: Yale University Press, 1973.

Danielsen, Albert L. The Evolution of OPEC. New York: Harcourt Brace Jovanovich, 1982.

Dixon, C.J., D. Drakakis-Smith, and H.D. Watts, eds. Multinational Corporations and the Third World. Boulder: Westview Press, 1986.

Dos Santos, Theotonio. "The Structure of Dependence," in K. T. Fann and Donald C. Hodges, eds., Readings in U.S. Imperialism. Boston, Mass.: Porter Sargent Publishers, 1971.

Dunning, John H. The Multinational Enterprise. London: George Allen and Unwin Ltd., 1971.

The Economist. The World in Figures. New York: Facts on File, Inc., 1980.

Ekstein, Harry. "Case Study and Theory in Political Science," in Fred I. Greenstein and Nelson W. Polsby, eds., Handbook of Political Science, Volume 7: Strategies of Inquiry. Reading, Mass.: Addison-Wesley, 1975.

Evans, Peter. Dependent Development: The Alliance of Multinational, State, and Local Capital in Brazil. Princeton: Princeton University Press, 1979.

Farrell, Trevor M. A. "The Multinational Corporation, the Petroleum Industry and Economic Underdevelopment in Trinidad and Tobago." Ph.D. dissertation, Cornell University, 1974.

Frank, André Gunder. "The Development of Underdevelopment," in James D. Cockcroft, André Gunder Frank, and Dale L. Johnson, Dependence and Underdevelopment: Latin America's Political Economy. New York: Anchor Books, 1972.

Frank, Isaiah. Foreign Enterprise in Developing Countries. Baltimore: Johns Hopkins Press, 1980.

Girvan, Norman. Corporate Imperialism: Conflict and Expropriation. White Plains, New York: M.E. Sharpe Inc., 1976.

Goodsell, Charles T. American Corporations and Peruvian Politics. Cambridge, Mass.: Harvard University Press, 1974.

Hartshorn, J.E. Politics and World Economics. New York: Praeger Publishers, 1967.

Henry, Zin. Labour Relations and Industrial Conflict in Commonwealth Caribbean Countries. Port-of-Spain, Trinidad and Tobago: Columbus Publishers Ltd., 1972.

Hewlett, Sylvia A. The Cruel Dilemmas of Development: Twentieth Century Brazil. New York: Basic Books, 1980.

Jacoby, Neil H. Multinational Oil: A Study in Industrial Dynamics. New York: Macmillan Publishing Co., Inc. 1974.

Keohane, Robert, and Joseph Nye, eds. Transnational Relations and World Politics. Cambridge, Mass.: Harvard University Press, 1972.

Kindleberger, Charles P., and David B. Audretsch, eds. The Multinational Corporation in the 1980s. Cambridge, Mass.: MIT Press, 1983.

Mahabir, Winston. In and Out of Politics. Trinidad: Inprint Caribbean Ltd., 1975.

Malik, Yogendra K. East Indians in Trinidad: A Study in Minority Politics. London: Oxford University Press, 1971.

Mericle, Kenneth S. "Corporations Control of the Working Class: Brazil Since 1964," in James M. Malloy, ed., Authoritarianism and Corporatism in Latin America. Pittsburgh: University of Pittsburgh Press, 1977.

Mikesell, Raymond F. "Conflict in Foreign Investor-Host Country Relations: A Preliminary Analysis," in Raymond F. Mikesell, ed., Foreign Investment in the Petroleum and Mineral Industries: Case Studies of Investor-Host Country Relations. Baltimore: Johns Hopkins Press, 1971.

Moran, Theodore H. Multinational Corporations and the Politics of Dependence: Copper in Chile. Princeton: Princeton University Press, 1974.

---. "The Theory of International Exploitation in Large Natural Resource Investments," in Steven J. Rosen and James P. Kurth, eds., Testing Theories of Economic Imperialism. Lexington, Mass.: D.C. Heath and Company, 1973.

Oxaal, Ivar. Race and Revolutionary Consciousness: A Documentary Interpretation of the 1970 Black Power Revolt in Trinidad. Cambridge, Mass.: Schenkman Publishing Company, Inc., 1971.

---. Black Intellectuals Come to Power: The Rise of Creole Nationalism in Trinidad and Tobago. Cambridge, Mass.: Schenkman Publishing Company, Inc., 1968.

Penrose, Edith T. The Large International Firm in Developing Countries: The International Petroleum Industry. Cambridge, Mass.: MIT Press, 1968.

Pinelo, Adalberto J. The Multinational Corporation as a Force in Latin American Politics: A Case Study of the International Petroleum Company in Peru. New York: Praeger Publishers, 1973.

Robinson, A.N.R. The Mechanics of Independence: Patterns of Political and Economic Transformation in Trinidad and Tobago. Cambridge, Mass.: MIT Press, 1971.

Rostow, W. W. The Stages of Economic Growth: A Non-Communist Manifesto. Cambridge: Cambridge University Press, 1965.

Ryan, Selwyn D. Race and Nationalism in Trinidad and Tobago: A Case Study of Decolonization in a Multiracial Society. Toronto: University of Toronto Press, 1972.

Seers, Dudley. "The Stages of Economic Growth of a Primary Producer in the Middle of the Twentieth Century," in Robert I. Rhodes, ed., Imperialism and Underdevelopment: A Reader. New York: Monthly Review Press, 1970.

Sigmund, Paul E. Multinationals in Latin America: The Politics of Nationalization. Madison: University of Wisconsin Press, 1980.

Smith, David N., and Louis T. Wells. Negotiating Third World Mineral Agreements: Promises as Prologue. Cambridge, Mass.: Ballinger Publishing Co., 1975.

Stone, Carl. Stratification and Political Change in Trinidad and Jamaica. Beverly Hills, Calif.: Sage Publications, 1972.

Tughendat, Christopher, and Adrian Hamilton. Oil: The Biggest Business. London: Eyre Methuen Ltd., 1975.

Tugwell, Franklin. The Politics of Oil in Venezuela. Stanford: Stanford University Press, 1975.

United Nations. <u>Yearbook of International Trade Statistics</u>. New York: The United Nations, 1965-1982.

Vernon, Raymond. <u>Storm Over the Multinationals: The Real Issues</u>. Cambridge, Mass.: Harvard University Press, 1977.

Wallerstein, Immanuel. <u>The Capitalist World-Economy</u>. Cambridge: Cambridge University Press, 1979.

Williams, Eric E. <u>Inward Hunger: The Education of a Prime Minister</u>. London: André Deutsch, 1969.

---. <u>History of the People of Trinidad and Tobago</u>. Port-of-Spain, Trinidad: PNM Publishing Co., Ltd., 1962.

The World Bank. <u>World Tables, Volume I</u>. Baltimore: Johns Hopkins University Press, 1976.

---. <u>World Tables, Volume I</u>. Baltimore: Johns Hopkins University Press, 1980.

---. <u>World Tables, Volume I</u>. Baltimore: Johns Hopkins University Press, 1983.

---. <u>World Tables, Volume II</u>. Baltimore: Johns Hopkins University Press, 1983.

---. <u>World Development Report, 1981</u>. New York: Oxford University Press, 1986.

ARTICLES

Bodenheimer, Susanne. "Dependency and Imperialism: The Roots of Latin America Underdevelopment," <u>Politics and Society</u> 1 (May 1971), 327-357.

Burdette, Marcia M. "Nationalization in Zambia: A Critique of Bargaining Theory," <u>Canadian Journal of African Studies</u> 11 (1977), 417-496.

Chilcote, Ronald H. "A Question of Dependency," <u>Latin American Research Review</u> 13 (1978), 55-66.

Chirot, Daniel, and Thomas Hall. "World-System Theory," <u>Annual Review of Sociology</u> 8 (1982), 81-106.

Curry, Robert L., Jr., and Donald Rothchild. "On Economic Bargaining between African Governments and Multinational Companies," The Journal of Modern African Studies 12 (1974), 173-189.

Diebold, John. "Multinational Corporations. . . Why Be Scared of Them?" Foreign Policy 12 (Fall 1973), 79-95.

Grieco, Joseph M. "Between Dependency and Autonomy: India's Experience with the International Computer Industry," International Organization 30 (Summer 1982), 609-632.

Johnson, Caswell. "Political Unionism and the Collective Objective in Economies of British Colonial Origin: The Cases of Jamaica and Trinidad," American Journal of Economics and Sociology 34 (October 1975), 365-379.

Keohane, Robert. "Lilliputians' Dilemmas: Small States in International Politics," International Organization 23 (Spring 1969), 291-311.

Leonard, Jeffrey. "Multinational Corporations and Politics in Developing Countries," World Politics 32 (April 1980), 454-483.

Malik, Yogendra K. "Socio-political Perceptions and Attitudes of East Indian Elites in Trinidad," The Western Political Quarterly 23 (September 1970), 552-563.

Moran, Theodore H. "Multinational Corporations and Dependency: A Dialogue for Dependentistas and Non-dependentistas," in James A. Caporaso, ed., Dependence and Dependency in the Global System, special issue of International Organization 30 (Winter 1978), 178-200.

NACLA. "Oil in the Caribbean: Focus on Trinidad," Latin America and Empire Report 10 (October 1976), 1-32.

Nichols, David G. "East Indians and Black Power in Trinidad," Race 12 (April 1971), 443-459.

Ramlogan, Vishnu. "The Sugar Industry in Trinidad and Tobago: Management: Challenges and Responses," Inter-American Economic Affairs 33 (Spring 1980), 29-59.

Ray, David. "The Dependency Model of Latin American Underdevelopment: Three Basic Fallacies," Journal of Inter-American Studies and World Affairs (February 1973), 4-20.

Root, Franklin R. "Foreign Government Constraints on U.S. Business Abroad," Economic and Business Bulletin 20 (September 1967), 28-37.

Ryan, Selwyn. "Trinidad and Tobago: The Transition from Anarchy to Republic," The Parliamentarian 58 (July 1979), 153-163.

Seers, Dudley. "Model of an Open Petroleum Economy," Social and Economic Studies 12 (June 1964), 233-242.

Spackman, Ann. "Constitutional Development in Trinidad and Tobago," Social and Economic Studies 14 (December 1965), 283-320.

Spengler, J.J. "Small Island Economies: Some Limitations," The South Atlantic Quarterly 70 (Winter 1971), 49-61.

OFFICIAL DOCUMENTS AND PUBLICATIONS (TRINIDAD)

"An Act to Amend the Petroleum Taxes Act, 1974," speech by the Minister of Energy and Energy-based Industries, Second Reading of the Bill, April 22, 1981.

Fourth Session Second Parliament Trinidad and Tobago, 18 Elizabeth II, Act no. 46 of 1969.

Third Session Third Parliament Trinidad and Tobago, 21 Elizabeth II, Act no. 23 of 1972, The Industrial Relations Act.

Third Session Third Parliament Trinidad and Tobago, 23 Elizabeth II, Act no. 22 of 1974.

Fifth Session First Parliament Republic of Trinidad and Tobago, Act no. 5 of 1981.

Boopsingh, Trevor M. "The Petroleum Industry--The Next Decade," Ministry of Energy and Energy-based Industries, Trinidad and Tobago, January 1, 1980.

Caroni Limited. Directors Reports and Accounts. Port-of-Spain, Trinidad: Caroni Limited, 1977.

Central Bank of Trinidad and Tobago. Monthly Statistical Digest 14 (September 1981).

Central Statistical Office. Annual Statistical Abstract. Port-of-Spain, Trinidad: Central Statistical Office Printing Unit, 1961-1985.

Government of Trinidad and Tobago. Conference Report on Best Uses of Our Petroleum Resources, vol. 1. Port-of-Spain, Trinidad: Government Printery (undated).

---. Pioneer Manufacturers Statistical Studies and Papers 8. Port-of-Spain, Trinidad: Government Printery, 1961.

---. Third Five-Year Plan 1969-1973 as Approved by Parliament. Port-of-Spain, Trinidad: Government Printery, 1969.

---. Accounting for the Petrodollar. Port-of-Spain, Trinidad: Government Printery, 1980.

---. Accounting for the Petrodollar 1973-1983. Port-of-Spain, Trinidad: Government Printery, 1984.

Industrial Development Corporation. Why Foreign Investment is Attracted to Trinidad and Tobago. Port-of-Spain, Trinidad: Yuille Printery Limited, 1962.

Ministry of Energy. History of Oil in Trinidad. (undated).

Ministry of Finance. Report of Fiscal Review Committee. Port-of-Spain, Trinidad: Government Printery, 1981.

"The Petroleum Regulations, 1970." Supplement to the Trinidad and Tobago Gazette 9 (February 19, 1970).

Public Relations Division, Prime Minister's Office, Whitehall, Trinidad. Facts on Trinidad and Tobago. Port-of-Spain, Trinidad: Government Printery, 1977.

Report of the Commission of Inquiry into Subversive Activities in Trinidad and Tobago. Port-of-Spain, Trinidad: Government Printery, 1965.

Republic of Trinidad and Tobago. Report of the Committee to Review Government Exenditure. Port-of-Spain, Trinidad: Government Printery, 1978.

---. Report of the Committee to Consider the Rationalization of the Sugar Industry, Vol. 1 and 2. Port-of-Spain, Trinidad: The Government Printery, 1979.

---. Review of the Economy. Trinidad and Tobago: Central Statistical Office Printing Unit, 1978-1986.

Trinidad Tesoro Company Limited. Annual Report 1978. Port-of-Spain, Trinidad: College Press, 1979.

MONOGRAPHS AND PAMPHLETS

Farrell, Trevor M.A. "In Whose Interest: Nationalization and Bargaining with the Petroleum Multinationals: The Trinidad and Tobago Experience," in Proceedings of the Conference on Contemporary Trends and Issues in Caribbean International Affairs. St. Augustine, Trinidad: Institute of International Relations, University of the West Indies, 1977.

Jacobs, Richard W. "Factors Affecting Trade Union Organization and Development in Trinidad and Tobago," in W. Richard Jacobs et al., Seminar on Contemporary Issues, No. 1: Labor and Industrial Relations in Trinidad and Tobago. Trinidad and Tobago: Faculty of Social Sciences, University of the West Indies, 1971.

Parris, Carl D. Capital of Labor? The Decision to Introduce the Industrial Stabilization Act in Trinidad and Tobago: Working Paper No. 2. Jamaica: Institute of Social and Economic Research, University of the West Indies, 1965.

Thomas, R.D. "The Next Step in Industrial Relations in Trinidad and Tobago," in W. Richard Jacobs et al., Seminar on Contemporary Issues, No. 1: Labor and Industrial Relations in Trinidad and Tobago. Trinidad and Tobago: Faculty of Social Sciences, University of the West Indies, 1971.

UNPUBLISHED SOURCES

Blowers, Charles William. "The Industrial Development of Trinidad, 1952-1962." M.A. thesis, University of Florida, June 1964.

Ryan, Selwyn. "The Disunited Labor Front" (unpublished paper), 1978.

Sudama, Trevor. "Class, Race and the State in Trinidad and Tobago" (unpublished paper).

TRADE UNION AND POLITICAL PARTY LITERATURE

Address by Mr. Karl T. Hudson-Phillips at the inaguration of the Organization for National Reconstruction on Sunday, February 1, 1981, at the Chaguaramas Convention Center.

Alliance: Policy and Programme. San Fernando, Trinidad: Rahaman Printery Ltd., 1981.

Lequay, Alloy. "The Democratic Labor Party: The Struggle for Unity, 1968-1975" (undated).

OWTU. Oil in Turmoil and OWTU Memorandum on the Formation of a National Oil Company. San Fernando, Trinidad: Vanguard Publishing Company, Ltd., 1967.

---. Oilfields Workers' Trade Union, July 1937-July 1977. Trinidad and Tobago: Syncreators Ltd., 1977.

PNM. General Elections 1966: Manifesto, Port-of-Spain, Trindad: PNM Publishing Company Ltd. (undated).

---. Perspectives for the New Society: People's Charter 1956 (revised).

---. PNM Manifesto, 1981 General Elections: The First Twenty-Five Years. Trinidad and Tobago: Trinidad and Tobago Printing and Packaging Limited, 1981.

"Programme for Change: ONR Manifesto", Elections 1981. Sunday Guardian Advertising Supplement, October 25, 1981.

"Twenty Years is Enough", United Labour Front: Elections Manifesto 1976. Curepe, Trinidad: Truprint (undated).

NEWSPAPERS

Caribbean Contact

Express

Trinidad Guardian

INDEX

Action Committee of Dedicated Citizens
[ACDC], 58
Africans. See Blacks
Aid to Pioneer Industries Ordinance
[1950], 65, 105
Amoco Trinidad Oil Company: begins
operations, 31; and crude oil development, 39, 42, 44, 105; dominance of,
97, 111; and employment, 106; explorations of, 43, 101, 106, 116-17;
government relations with, 97, 98,
105-6, 111-12, 114, 117, 118-19; and
marine petroleum, 34, 35, 36, 37, 42,
43, 44, 90, 104, 105, 115, 116-17; marketing by, 42, 112; and the OWTU,
106; production at, 35-37, 44, 105-6;
refining operations at, 42, 105-6; and
taxes, 99; and Trinidad Tesoro, 104,
112
ATSEFWTU [All-Trinidad Sugar Estates
and Factory Workers' Trade Union]:
founding of, 51; government relations
with the, 62, 98, 114; and the Industrial Stabilization Act [1965], 68-69;
and labor politics, 53; leadership of
the, 74; and Marxism/socialism, 68-
69, 78; and nationalization of the
sugar industry, 72, 74, 98, 114; sugar
industry relations with the, 74-75;

and the ULF, 113; wage demands by
the, 74-75. See also Caroni Ltd.;
inter-ethnic coalition

bargaining: and dependency, 119-21;
and domestic politics, 7, 9, 13, 45,
92, 112, 121; dynamic, 5; and essentiality, 9-11; and expertise, 11,
120-21; factors in, 121; government's position in, 87, 92, 96, 107,
112, 115, 116, 117, 118, 120-21; and
incentives, 12-13; and marine petroleum, 37; MNCs' position/pressures
in, 86, 115, 118, 119; motivations of
host country in, 12-14; and nationalism, 8, 13; and nationalization,
6, 8-9, 12, 107; and oil prices, 96,
107, 115, 117, 120, 122; and oil
reserves, 121; reasons for, 12; and
renegotiation, 6-7, 8; and risk, 11,
116; static, 5-6; and taxes, 115, 120-
121; theories about, 4-9, 119-21
Black Power revolution [1969-70], 61-
62, 71-73, 74, 79, 91, 92, 93-94, 113,
114
blacks: dominance of, 48; occupations
of, 48-49; political consciousness of,
50-53; population of, 50. See also
Black Power revolution; ethnicity;

inter-ethnic coalition; racism;
name of specific topic or person
Bloody Tuesday [1975], 77
brain drain, 34
Britain, 48, 50, 54-55, 62. See also
British Petroleum Trinidad Ltd.
British Petroleum Trinidad Ltd.:
acquisition of, 2, 43, 59, 87-90,
100, 107, 114, 118, 119; compensation to, 88; and domestic politics,
47; and employment, 84, 87-88; and
the expertise issue, 88, 89; and
explorations, 86, 87; founding of,
31, 84; and the industrialization
effort, 86-87; production at, 87,
116; strike against, 84; and TNA,
37; and Trinidad Tesoro, 36
British West Indian Airways [BWIA],
23, 106-7
Butler, Tubal Uriah, 50-51, 53, 54, 62

Capildeo, Rudranath N., 55-56, 57-58,
64
Caribbean National Labor Party
[CNLP], 53-54, 63, 68
Caribbean Socialist Party, 51
Caroni Ltd., 47, 69, 73, 75-76, 86-87,
93, 98-99, 106-7, 114, 119
Cipriani, Andrew, 50, 53
class issue, 61, 70-71, 75, 77-78, 92, 113
colonialism, 48-51, 62
communism, 67-68, 69, 77, 113
compensation, 11, 88, 95-96, 102, 105,
106, 116
concessions process, 3-9, 65-66. See also
bargaining
crude oil, 20, 37, 39-40, 42, 45, 85-86,
90, 102, 112, 114. See also taxes;
name of specific oil company
Curry, Robert L., 5-6

Daaga, Makandal. See Granger, Geddes
Democratic Action Congress [DAC], 78
Democratic Liberation Party, 58
demonstrations, 64, 69, 71-72, 98, 100.
See also strikes
dependency: and an oil policy, 45; and
bargaining, 119-21; and constraints
on industry, 44, 87; and crude oil
development, 45; and expertise avail-

ability, 45, 111-12, 116, 117, 120;
and explorations, 44, 45; and marine
petroleum, 37-38; and marketing,
45, 117; and nationalization, 3-5,
45, 112, 118, 119-21; on the oil
industry, 45, 76, 91, 111-12, 119;
and oil prices, 111, 120; and production, 45; and refining operations,
45, 112; on the sugar industry, 91,
119; theories about, 3-5, 119-21.
See also name of specific oil
company
DLP [Democratic Labor Party], 54,
55-58, 59, 61-62, 64-65, 75, 77-78,
113. See also elections
domestic politics: and bargaining, 7,
9, 13, 45, 92, 112, 121; and ethnicity, 58-59; and the federal elections, 54-55; MNC's as an issue in,
111-22; MNCs' insulation from, 47-
48; and nationalization, 79; and
political mobilization, 48-52; and
racism, 47-59; and taxes, 120; and
the two-party system, 52-54. See
also elections; name of specific
company, political party, or topic

economic nationalism, 6, 8, 9, 13, 47,
79, 83-107, 114-15, 116, 119
economic planning, 45, 91
elections: of 1946, 51, 52; of 1950,
51, 52, 62; of 1956, 52, 53-54, 63,
68; of 1958, 54-55, 56, 63; of 1961,
56, 63, 64, 67; of 1966, 57, 70-71; of
1971, 58, 97; of 1976, 58, 75, 77-78,
113; of 1981, 78; of 1986, 78; and
the class issue, 92; and electoral
boundaries, 56; and ethnicity/
racism, 55, 56, 63, 64-65, 71, 78;
federal, 54-55, 56, 63; reform of, 58;
and the trade unions, 62, 63, 67,
92; and voter registration, 56; and
voting machines, 56
electoral boundaries, 56, 57
employment: and the Five-Year Plan,
91; and the industrialization effort,
86-87; and nationalization, 107;
and the oil industry, 23, 84, 85, 89;
overview of, 23-27; and patronage/
special works program, 23, 26, 48,

56-57, 91, 107; and the sugar industry, 93; and the Texaco acquisition, 103. See also name of specific company
essential industries, 74, 113
essentiality, 9-11, 28, 45, 111, 116, 117
ethnicity; and the class issue, 61, 75, 113; and colonialism, 50; and domestic politics, 50-51, 55, 56, 58-59, 63, 64-65, 70, 71, 78, 112-13; and elections, 55, 56, 64-65, 71, 78; historical aspects of, 48; and the ISA, 70; and nationalization, 61, 113; and the oil industry, 61; political consciousness, 50-51; and political parties, 52, 54, 55, 61, 78, 112-13; and the sugar industry, 61; and the trade unions, 51, 59, 61, 78-79
expertise: and bargaining, 11, 120-21; and the brain drain, 34; and the British Petroleum acquisition, 88-89; and dependency, 111-12, 116, 117, 120; and economic planning, 91; and educational facilities, 33; and explorations, 43, 44, 112, 116; government programs to develop, 34; and land petroleum, 111; and marine petroleum, 34, 37, 44, 111; and marketing, 116; and nationalization, 11, 12, 37, 116; and oil reserves, 33, 86, 116, 117; and production, 37, 116, 117
exploration, 43-45, 85, 90, 112, 115, 116, 117, 118. See also taxes; name of specific company
exports, 20, 42

Farquhar, Peter, 57, 71
federal elections, 54-55, 56, 63
Federal Labor Party, 54-55
Five-Year Plan [1969-73], 91
foreign investors, 12-13, 65, 85-86, 87, 112, 118, 120. See also MNCs; name of specific company
Frank, André Gunder, 3
fuel oil, 41-42, 95, 105
FWTU [Federated Workers' Trade Union], 62, 63

gasoline, domestic, 42-43, 102, 103, 114
GDP [gross domestic product], 18-20, 111
general welfare, 26-28, 45, 118
Girvan, Norman, 3-4, 9
GNP [gross national product], 17-18
Gowandan, Krishna, 68-69
Granger, Geddes, 71-72

Hewlett, Sylvia Ann, 9
Houlder, Joseph, 67
Hudson-Phillips, Karl, 78
Huntington, Samuel P., 1

imports, crude oil, 39-40, 102, 112, 114
incentives, 12-13, 65
Indians: and the Black Power revolution, 72, 92; and the indentured system, 48, 92; occupations of, 48-49; political consciousness of, 50-51; population of, 50. See also DLP; ethnicity; inter-ethnic coalition; PDP; racism; sugar industry
industrialization effort, 65-66, 67, 85-86, 88, 112
Industrial Relations Act [1972], 73-74, 113
Industrial Stabilization Act [1965], 68-71, 73-74, 85-86, 92-93, 113
inter-ethnic coalition, 61-62, 68-71, 74-76, 78-79, 106, 113, 114
international oil industry, 18, 45, 84, 94, 120, 122. See also oil prices
Iron and Steel Company of Trinidad and Tobago [ISCOTT], 23, 106-7
Island-Wide Cane Farmers' Trade Union [ICFTU], 75

Jamadar, Vernon, 57, 58
James, C.L.R., 68, 70

Keohane, Robert, 14
Kern Trinidad Oilfieds, 31

labor: control of, 85-86, 112, 113, 114; costs of, 93; in the early 1960s, 66-68; economic nationalism, 9; ethnicity, 51; industrialization

effort, 66; and politics, 9, 51, 53-54; and self-government, 62
labor, See employment; trade unions; name of specific union
land petroleum, 37, 84, 85, 87, 89, 102, 111, 117. See also name of specific company
Lasalle, Rex, 72
Leonard, Winston, 72
Lequay, Alloy, 58
Lewis, W. A., 65, 66
Liberal Party, 57
Lindon, George, 62

Maharaj, Stephen, 57, 68, 70, 71
Malik, Yogendra, 56
Manley, Norman, 54
Maraj, Bhadase Sagan, 53, 54, 55, 58, 68-69
marine petroleum, 34, 36-38, 41-42, 44, 85, 90, 102, 106, 111, 115, 117. See also name of specific company
marketing, 12, 41-45, 86-87, 89, 112, 116, 117. See also taxes; name of specific company
Marxism, 3-4, 67-68, 77, 119-20. See also name of specific person
Mericle, Kenneth, 9
Mikesell, Raymond, 6-7, 9
MNCs [multinational corporations]: advantages/disadvantages of, 1-2, 13-14; bargaining position of, 4-9, 12, 13, 115; criticisms of, 2; dominance of, 94, 121; as exploiters, 62; growth of, 1; viewpoints about, 1-2. See also name of specific company or topic
mobilization: nationalization as a strategy for, 61-79, 107
Mobil Oil Corporation, 43
Moran, Theodore, 7-8, 11, 37, 119, 120-21
Mustofi Commission Report [1964], 33, 85-86, 89, 90

NAR [National Alliance for Reconstruction], 78, 105, 106
nationalism. See economic nationalism
nationalization: and bargaining, 6, 8-9, 12, 107; and the Black Power

revolution, 79, 91, 94, 113, 114; and capitalism, 4; decline of, 79, 98; demonstrations/strikes, 98; and dependency, 3-5, 45, 112, 118, 119-21; deterrents to, 10-12, 44-45, 116; and domestic politics, 79; and employment, 107; and ethnicity, 61, 113; and expertise availability, 11, 12, 37, 116; failure of, 83, 106-7, 117, 119; government commitment to, 2, 75-76; and the inter-ethnic coalition, 61-62, 74-76, 79, 106, 113, 114; and the ISA, 70; and marine petroleum, 37-38; and marketing, 12, 41, 44; as a mobilization strategy, 61-79, 107; necessity of, 4; of the oil industry, 37, 44-45, 54, 63, 72, 79, 84, 94, 98; and oil prices, 79, 107; as a piecemeal process, 83, 89, 106, 114; and production; reasons for, 83; and risk, 11-12; and socialism, 79; and subsidizations, 106-7; of the sugar industry, 72, 76, 98, 106, 113, 114, 119; of the Texaco refinery, 39-40; and the trade unions, 63, 87-88, 113; of utilities, 57. See also compensation; name of specific company or industry
National Petroleum Marketing Company [NPMC], 42-43
National Trade Union Congress [NTUC], 64, 67-68, 69
National Union of Government Employees, 67-68
NJAC [National Joint Action Council], 71-72, 92, 93-94

Occidental Petroleum Corporation, 43
O'Connor, Quintin, 68
offshore oil. See marine petroleum
O'Hallaran, John, 88
oil industry: and bargaining, 86, 119; and Blacks, 49, 79, 94; and demonstrations/strikes, 50-51, 75, 84, 98; and dependency, 45, 76, 91, 111-12, 119; and domestic politics, 47, 122; dominance of, 18-20, 122; and economic growth, 45; and employment,

23, 37, 84, 85, 89; and essentiality, 28, 45, 111; and ethnicity, 61; and expertise availability, 37; exports of the, 20; government relations with the, 83-87, 94, 97; growth in, 20; history of, 31; and the industrialization effort, 66, 86-87; inquiry into the, 84-85; and the international petroleum economy, 18, 94; nationalization of the, 37, 44-45, 54, 63, 72, 79, 84, 94, 98; organization of the, 33-44; and political parties, 59; public attitudes about the, 33; and subsidization of other sectors of the economy, 3, 23, 27, 28, 45, 76, 83, 98, 111, 114, 118; and taxes, 90, 91-92, 96-98, 99-100, 107, 115; and wages, 84, 93. See also OWTU; name of specific company or topic
oil policy, 45, 59. See also Mustofi Commission Report; name of specific legislation
oil prices: and bargaining, 96, 107, 115, 117, 120, 122; and the Caroni acquisition, 93; and decline in the oil industry, 87; and dependency, 111, 120; and domestic politics, 74; and explorations, 43; and fuel oil, 42; and gasoline, 43; and GNP/GDP, 18-20; and government control of industry, 94; and nationalization, 79, 107; and refining operations, 39; and the Shell acquisition, 95; and taxes, 97, 118; and the Texaco acquisition, 102-3
oil reserves, 33, 39-40, 84, 85, 86, 89, 111, 116, 117, 119, 121
ONR [Organization for National Reconstruction], 78
OPEC, 39, 74, 96, 103, 120
OWTU [Oilfields Workers' Trade Union]: and elections, 63; and the Black Power revolution, 71, 72, 91, 113; demands of, 84; and economic nationalism, 47, 62-63; and ethnicity, 59; founding of, 51, 62; imprisonment of leaders of, 73; and the industrialization effort, 67; internal discord in the, 67; investigation of the, 67-68, 113; and the Mustofi Commission Report, 85; and nationalization, 54, 72, 79, 84, 87-88; and the NTUC, 64, 70; and political parties, 59; power of the, 68, 70, 73; and racism, 72; and representation of other worker categories by the, 73; socialism/communism, 61-62, 78, 113; and strikes, 75; and the TTEC, 73; and the ULF, 113; and the WFP, 70-71; and the WIIP, 68. See also inter-ethnic coalition; name of specific company or person
Oxaal, Ivar, 53

Panday, Basdeo, 70, 71, 74-75, 77, 78
patronage. See employment
PDP [People's Democratic Party] 48, 53, 54. See also Democratic Labor Party; elections
Penrose, Edith, 43
Petroleum Act [1969], 85, 90, 97, 105, 115, 118
petroleum engineers, 33, 117
petroleum inspectors, 34, 117
Petroleum Regulations, 90
Petroleum Taxes Act [1974], 96-98, 99, 103-4, 115, 117, 118. See also Supplemental Petroleum Tax
Pierre, Lennox, 68, 70, 71, 77
pioneer industries, 65-66, 105
PNM [People's National Movement] government. See name of specific topic or person
PNM [People's National Movement] party: as the Black party, 52, 61; criticism of, 53; ethnicity, 58-59, 63; fear of the, 53; and the federal elections, 54; and the Federal Labor Party, 55; founding of, 52, 53; and racism, 48; splits within the, 58. See also elections; name of specific topic
political consciousness, 50-53
Political Education Group. See PNM
political parties, 51-52, 53-54, 55, 59, 61-62, 112-13. See also name of specific party

Political Progress Group, 51
political unions. See trade unions;
   name of specific union
POPPG [Party of Political Progress
   Groups], 53, 54, 57. See also
   Democratic Labor Party; Liberal
   Party
Premier Consolidated, 35
Primus, Bernard, 100
production, 33-38, 39, 44, 45, 85, 86, 90,
   93, 116, 117. See also taxes; name
   of specific company
public utilities, 57

race issues, 47-59, 63, 72, 92. See also
   ethnicity; inter-ethnic coalition
Ramnath, Kelvin, 43, 106
refining operations, 20, 38-42, 44, 45,
   85, 87, 90, 112. See also taxes;
   name of specific company
Ridley, Robert, 106
Rienzi, Adrian Cola, 50, 51, 62, 68-
   69, 70
risk, 11-12, 43, 112, 116, 117
Robinson, A.N.R., 58, 78
Rojas, John, 54, 62, 63, 64, 67, 68
Rothchild, Donald, 5-6
Rouhani, Fuad, 90
Ryan, Selwyn, 52, 53, 56

Seamen and Waterfront Workers'
   Trade Union. See SWWTU
Shah, Raffique, 72, 75, 77
Shell Trinidad Ltd.: acquisition of,
   2, 36, 43, 94-96, 97, 100, 107,
   114, 117, 119; begins operations,
   31; and the British Petroleum
   acquisition, 87, 88, 118; compensation to, 95-96; and crude oil,
   95; and domestic politics, 47;
   and employment, 84, 87, 95; and
   exploration, 86, 95; and the industrialization effort, 86-87; and
   land production, 87; and marketing, 87; production operations
   of, 95, 116; refining operations
   of, 95; and TNA, 37. See also
   TRINTOC
Sigmund, Paul, 5, 11
Sinanan, Ashford, 53, 55

Sinanan, Mitra, 53
slavery, 48, 53, 92
Smith, David N., 6, 45
socialism, 50, 55, 57, 61-62, 70-71, 78,
   79. See also name of specific
   person
Southern Workers' Trade Union, 63
special works program, 23, 26, 56, 91
standard of living, 26-27, 111, 118
state of emergency, 56, 61, 64, 70, 73
strikes: DLP position on, 64; increase
   in, 66-67; and the inter-ethnic coalition, 75; legal restrictions on, 57,
   61, 69-70, 71, 73-74, 113; in the oil
   industry, 50-51, 84; and the public
   transportation system, 71; reasons
   for, 67; and self-government, 62;
   and the sugar industry, 69, 75. See
   also demonstrations
subsidization: of gas stations, 43; of the
   general welfare, 23, 26-27, 45, 118;
   and nationalization, 106-7; oil
   industry as a source of, 3, 23, 27,
   28, 45, 76, 83, 98, 111, 114, 118; of
   the sugar industry, 23, 76, 114; of
   various companies, 23
subversive activities. See communism
sugar cane farmers, 75
sugar industry: and bargaining, 119;
   and the Black Power revolution,
   79, 91, 114; and demonstrations/
   strikes, 69, 75, 98; and dependency,
   91, 119; and the DLP, 59; and
   domestic politics, 47; early development of, 48-49; and economic
   nationalism, 92; and employment, 93;
   and ethnicity, 61; and the industrialization effort, 66, 86-87; and
   the Industrialization Stabilization
   Act [1965], 68-69; labor costs in
   the, 93; losses in the, 23; and nationalization, 23, 72, 73, 74, 75-76,
   79, 91, 113, 114, 119; and the
   NJAC, 92; and the OWTU, 61, 92;
   PNM government, 92-94; and production, 93; subsidization of the,
   3, 23, 76, 83, 98, 114; and taxes,
   91-92; union relations with the, 74-
   75; wages in the, 23, 93. See also
   ATSEFWTU; Caroni Ltd.; inter-

ethnic coalition
sugar plantations, 47-48, 92
sugar union. See AFSEFWTU
Supplemental Petroleum Tax, 99-100,
  102, 104, 106, 118
SWWTU [Seamen and Waterfront
  Workers' Trade Union], 62, 69, 73

Tapia party, 78
Tate and Lyle Ltd., 73, 76, 98, 119
taxes: and bargaining, 115, 120-21;
  and the Black Power revolution,
  91-92; and domestic politics; 120;
  and the industrialization effort,
  65-66; MNCs' demands for
  revision of, 99-100, 115, 117, 118;
  and the oil industry, 90, 96-98, 99-
  100, 106, 107, 115; and oil prices,
  118. See also name of specific
  legislation
technology. See expertise
Tenneco Corporation, 43
Tesoro Petroleum Company of
  Texas. See Trinidad Tesoro Oil
  Company
Texaco Trinidad Inc.: acquisition of, 39-
  40, 74, 100-103, 107, 113-14, 118-19;
  and bargaining, 118; begins operations, 31, 84; and the British Petroleum acquisition, 87, 88, 118; and
  the commission of inquiry, 101-2;
  compensation to, 102; as a crude oil
  developer, 20, 39, 101, 102, 114;
  demonstrations/strikes against,
  75, 98, 100; dependency on, 20,
  39, 44, 112, 119; and the desulphurization plant, 42; domestic
  politics, 47, 100, 101; dominance
  of, 97, 111; and employment, 103,
  114; and expertise, 34; exploration,
  43, 101, 102; gas stations owned
  by, 43; government relations
  with, 97, 98, 100, 101; and the
  industrialization effort, 86-87;
  and land/marine petroleum, 102,
  103, 114; and marketing, 42, 112;
  and nationalization, 2, 100; and oil
  prices, 102-3; and the OWTU, 74, 100,
  101, 102; and production, 35-37, 86,
  100-101; refining operations at, 39-40,

42, 44, 86, 96-97, 100-103, 114; and
  taxes, 96-97, 99, 101, 115; and TNA,
  37; and TRINTOC, 101, 102
TNA. See Trinidad Northern Areas
Trades Union Council and Socialist
  Party, 63
Trade Union Congress, 51, 73
trade unions: and Blacks, 50-51, 91;
  and business unions, 62; and
  communism/Marxism, 67-69, 84-85;
  and the DLP, 61-62, 64; and elections, 62, 63, 67; and essential
  industries, 74; and ethnicity, 61,
  78-79; government relations with
  the, 57, 61, 63-65, 67; growth of,
  62; and the industrialization effort,
  66; and the ISA, 69-71; and nationalization, 63, 113; organization of
  the, 50; and political parties, 61-62;
  political power of the, 62-63; recognition of, 51, 67, 69-70, 74-75. See
  also inter-ethnic coalition; name
  of specific union
Transport and Industrial Workers'
  Union [TIWU], 71, 75
Trinidad: constitutional reforms in,
  51, 62; government structure of,
  17, 51, 52; history of, 17, 48; independence of, 47, 54-55, 57; as a
  materialistic society, 27; political
  mobilization in, 48-52; population
  of, 50; social structure in, 50.
  See also name of specific topic or
  person
Trinidad Canadian Oilfield, 35
Trinidad Island-Wide Cane Farmers'
  Association [TICFA], 74-75
Trinidad Labor Party [TLP], 50, 51,
  53, 54, 57. See also Democratic
  Labor Party; Liberal Party
Trinidad Leaseholds Limited, 31, 84
Trinidad Northern Areas [TNA], 35-
  37, 95, 102, 103
Trinidad Petroleum Development
  Company, 31, 84
Trinidad Tesoro Oil Company:
  acquisition of, 2, 44, 103-5, 107, 114,
  119; and British Petroleum, 36, 88-
  90, 118; compensation to, 105; and
  control of the oil industry, 97; and

crude oil, 42, 112; and employment, 37; and expertise, 88, 90; and exploration, 104; formation of, 36, 88-90; governmental relations with, 104; and land/marine petroleum, 39, 42, 104, 112; and marketing, 89, 90, 112; and production, 35-37; and refining operations, 39; and the Shell acquisition, 95; and taxes, 99, 103-4, 115; and the TNA, 37; and TRINTOC, 104, 112
Trinidad and Tobago Electricity Corporation [TTEC], 73
TRINTOC [Trinidad and Tobago Oil Company], 35-39, 42, 43, 44, 95, 100, 101, 102, 104, 112, 117
TTNA [Trinidad and Tobago National Alliance], 78
Tugwell, Franklin, 8-9, 28
Tull, Carl, 64

ULF [United Labor Front], 75, 76-78, 79, 98, 100, 101, 113, 114
unions. See trade unions; name of specific union or person

voter registration, 56
voting machines, 56

wages/working conditions, 23, 66, 67, 74, 77, 84, 93, 113
Wallerstein, Immanuel, 4
Weekes, George, 67, 68, 69, 70, 71, 72, 75, 77, 84
Wells, Louis T., Jr., 6, 45
West Indian Independence Party [WIIP], 67-68
West Indies Federation, 54-55
Williams, Eric Eustace, 52-53, 55, 56-57, 63, 64-65, 67, 69, 70, 72-73, 92
Workers' and Farmers' Party [WFP], 57, 70-71

Young, Joseph, 71

ABOUT THE AUTHOR

CHAITRAM SINGH is an assistant professor of political science at Berry College, Mt. Berry, Georgia. Born in Guyana, he holds a B.S. from the United States Military Academy at West Point, and an M.A. and Ph.D. from the University of Florida. He served as an officer of the Guyana Defense Force and was an assistant professor in the Department of Government and International Studies at the University of South Carolina. He is the author of <u>Guyana: Politics in a Plantation Society</u> (Praeger, 1988).